SPATIAL**PRACTICE**

Edited by Heather Woofter

Essays by Erdem Erten

Lynnette Widder

Stuart Steck

Chris Genter

ORO *editions*

Axi:Ome

ORO editions
Publishers of Architecture, Art, and Design
www.oroeditions.com   info@oroeditions.com

Copyright © 2009 by ORO editions

Color Separation and Printing: ORO editions Pte Ltd, Singapore

Library of Congress Catalogue Card Number ISBN: 978-0-9814628-5-1   Printed in China

ORO editions USA: PO Box 150338, San Rafael, CA 94915
ORO editions Asia: Block 8, Lorong Bakar Batu #02-04 Singapore 348743

Conception and Design: Axi:Ome llc: Sung Ho Kim

Design and Composition: Tina Yuan

Project Editor: Heather Woofter

Axi:Ome

Axi:Ome llc is committed to the development of new paradigms of spatial practice through issues of program, scale, technology and re-evaluating material regime through production of new forms of spatial configurations. We have adopted a non-linear design policy for flexibility within a design process that allows for spatial forms to mediate between multiple conditions and situations. These design systems, procedures, and architectural devices decode the emerging pattern recognition of a young practice in transition.

Axi:Ome llc practices architecture as a form of research, a complex form of cultural representation directly interfaced into social, economic and cultural influences. Media, technology and information have developed an unprecedented cultural shift, demanding reconsideration of the methods of current design strategies in architecture. In this accelerated culture of image and information, new technologies and media are the forces that distort the boundaries between public and private territories, between domestic and urban events and fields.

Axi:Ome llc challenges the boundaries between the physical and the virtual realms of design discipline, and researching the potential for new technologies that produce new programs and conditions. Axi:Ome llc emphasizes a critical ethos, developing architecture that projects awareness of shifting conditions and calibrates new design processes by deploying tectonic parameters of spatial materiality. This optimized design system is the ramification of expanding the field of architectural enterprise into new territories.

Axi:Ome llc is structured around the principle that a combination of specialized expertise and collaboration is the creative mode of operation. This approach has allowed the office to work in collaborative partnerships with a variety of architects, artists, graphic designers, media personnel, industrial designers, engineers, art historians, and developers on a wide spectrum of international projects.

Axi:Ome

This publication represents Sung Ho Kim's belief in architecture as a transformative experience. The works reside in the space between cultural critique and client-driven works of production, proving the capacity for architecture to exist as a creative act initiated by individual desire to ask questions and propose alternative ways of viewing the world.

Rosalind Krauss and Stan Allen have both described the research project as one that produces as well as transcribes. For an architect to provide insight into our world through visions of future possibilities, production resides at the core. When Sung Ho was working on his research degree, his advisors recommended that he begin a new kind of practice. It was clear that his speculations were of a material order.

This Spatial Practice emerged from the seeds of investigation at Massachusetts Institute of Technology, the Architectural Association of London and Rhode Island School of Design. Sung Ho was part of the first set of students to bridge the disciplines of aeronautical engineering and history/theory in architecture at MIT. His advisors and joint course materials inspired his ongoing work *Cartographing the Wind*. In addition, Sung Ho worked with Krzysztof Wodiczko developing robotics and bringing form to the technological interface between the body and physical and cultural voice. The AA contributed to his delicacy in urbanism and design strategies and RISD provided a foundation for experimentation and making.

Over the eight years following his work at MIT, Sung Ho has sought projects that resonate with critical frameworks that engage the digital and technological inventions of our minds, as well as the physically intimate artifacts of our body and senses. The process of production moves between articulate reiterative constructions of the hand and speculative geometries emerging from digital media. The conversation resides in the process work. This is not a monograph of individual buildings, but rather a way of seeking knowledge through making.

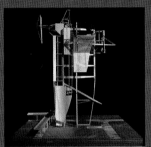

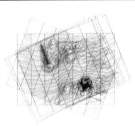

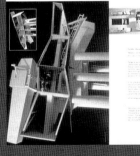

The name of the practice—Axi:Ome—is formed from two words, axiom and forme. Our visual world can pronounce and question with clarity in making.

The works of Axi:Ome rely on the generosity of supporters and the belief in architectural research projects as valuable education. Each of the works herein exists because of time and materials from a number of sponsors. Tina Yuan, a longtime friend of Axi:Ome, provides the graphic design. Students from Washington University in Saint Louis, Rhode Island School of Design, Northeastern University, Virginia Tech, Drury University and Kansas State University are dedicated collaborators. This influx of young talent creates a certain atmosphere where experimentation takes precedence over deliverable product. The work exists as research, yet within the liberation of un-built projects there is a belief in the precision of speculation.

Further, this volume demonstrates Sung Ho's flexibility: his work with industrial and graphic designers, media artists, landscape and urban designers, craft-artisans, theoreticians, engineers and architects assumes the role of partnership as opposed to consultation. Changing teams and circumstances gives voice to alternative methods of approach and discovery. In this way, Axi:Ome's spatial configuration literally moves with each project and these works are already the catalyst for the next shift in production. As an inspiring designer, educator and inventor, Sung Ho continues this conversation with multiple collaborators, all striving to give form to ideas.

From top to bottom: tower of babel international public design competition for nagoya, japan by sung ho kim with todd leong. cartographing the wind vectors and velocities of wind patterns by sung ho kim. *projective chronometry* by sung ho kim with tina yuan.

Axi:Ome

erdem erten

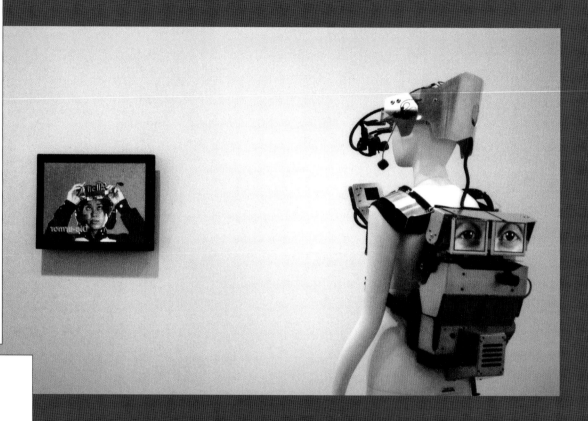

dis-armor version 3 interrogative design group with axi:ome llc. photo: Krysztof Wodiczko

on Axi:Ome llc's trajectory:

contextualizing program, programming context

In order to be able to give a fair evaluation of a young office such as Axi:Ome, one has to start with pointing to the ambitious array of design practices it performs and the underlining methodological basis that frames these practices. Axi:Ome's designs range from interactive multimedia, to sophisticated devices worn on the human body (such as their collaboration with Krzysztof Wodiczko), to digital analysis and reconstruction, and to larger scale architecture and urban design projects. Although every problem demands and generates a specific methodological approach, **the group's mode of operation always relies on process-oriented teamwork and an accompanying component of craft that links the conceptual to the constructional.** This short essay focuses mainly on the office's approach to architecture and urban design and comments on the use of digital media in their effort.

The late sixties can be regarded as the beginnings of **"contextualism,"** when Colin Rowe's studies at Cornell started to bear fruit and turned into a well-established design discourse.

By privileging urban form over the individual form of a building, contextualism criticized the modernist emphasis on the building being "an object in the round," as Thomas Schumacher called it.[i] In "Contextualism: Urban Ideals + Deformations," published in 1971, the problem of the modern city, identified with that of Le Corbusier's "city-in-the-park" — i.e. Ville Radieuse — was diagnosed as being a reversal of traditional urbanism. It favored clearly defined urban spaces that buildings conform to, instead of freestanding building volumes and empty spaces leftover from the building blocks. Still suffering from the avant-gardist assault on referencing history explicitly, Schumacher proposed contextualism as a middle ground between traditional and modern urbanism. However, he did not refrain from referring to contextualism as a formalist strategy. Urban form in the contextualist definition of Schumacher and Rowe was "seen as possessing a life of its own, irrespective of use, culture and economic conditions. Formal continuities therefore became an important consideration."[ii] The city is basically accepted as an autonomous formal entity that grows over time, and the architect has a very limited role in its development. The context of an urban intervention is therefore

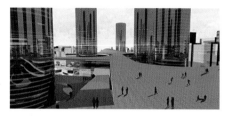
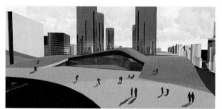
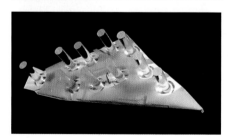

013 : osaka master plan

limited by the immediate peripheral conditions that define a site. The program is a given set of spaces and is accepted as a static entity. The architect has to come up with a solution that prioritizes the outer urban shell in possible arrangements that answer to the programmatic brief. This thinking is further

[i] Thomas Schumacher, "Contextualism: Urban Ideals + Deformations" *Casabella,* (1971): 359-60. [ii] Ibid., 81.

contextualizing program, programming context

reinforced by the analytical strategy and the problem-solving tools brought forward by the formalism inherent in the proposal. As Michael Hays states:

> Among his prescriptions ("stimulants" they are called) are (1) reconsider the dense texture of traditional cities such as Rome... (2) invert objects to obtain figurative voids, as Vasari's Uffizi palace is the inversion of Le Corbusier's Marseilles Unité (3) play "the long skinny building game," using continuous thin set pieces as "filters" or facades in order to discriminate certain conditions of building texture or landscape; (4) look to the French hotel for "habitable poché" and Soane's Bank of England for a collision of set pieces; (5) use "magically useless stabilizers" and "nostalgia producing instruments;" and reconstitute the urban garden.[iii]

Contextualism's most frequently utilized and most well known problem-solving tool among the above is **figure-ground** analysis. The pedagogy of the figure-ground has been employed in architectural schools all around the world in the last thirty years. As a tool it is and has been deceptively efficient in producing solutions for urban design problems. While the discouraging prospect of the twentieth-century experience instills a sense of nihilism in architects facing the uncontrollable urban dynamics, the widening of the rift between theory and practice reinforces this nihilism. **In this postmodern context of uncertainty and relativism, established strategies such as figure-ground become doubly effective by providing easy escape routes**, or should I just say quick answers? I do not aim to criticize all of the claims mentioned by the spokesmen of the discourse, but to point to the prevailing definition of contextualism established by them, to illuminate one strong agenda in Axi:Ome's design practice.

As effective as it can be, the kind of contextualism advocated by Rowe and Schumacher answers to a limited number of "contexts." As we can conclude from Hays' synopsis, it presupposes densely built urban environments (not only traditional European cities, of course) with its strategy of collage, or its calls for infill. It was also defined with reference to the avant-garde modernist schemes of the early

---

[iii] K. Michael Hays, ed. *Architectural Theory Since 1968* (MIT Press: Cambridge, 1999).

twentieth century that aimed to replace, not to develop or rehabilitate existing environments. So what if the "context" is not one of those mentioned in Hays' synopsis of Rowe? What about American suburbia, the edge city, the "technoburb", or declining industrial towns as potential problem sites to deal with? What if one starts with the definition of the word itself in order to generate different "contextualisms"? Can one propose or invent analytical tools for design that could be as helpful as the figure-ground and a strategy that would also allocate program as a more active role in the production of form? This is what Axi:Ome undertakes as its main problem for urban design.

The literal definition of the word 'context' points to an act of conjoining necessary for the emergence of a context. Hence, **context demands identification by way of revealing a "connected structure" within a "continuous text."** [iv] Thus, for the architect's use, context as a conceptual springboard presents multiple possibilities. It is an act demanded from the architect then, to survey the environment in order to arrive at, to separate, or to identify context. The architect has to map existing relationships and forecast those that are to be engendered. The limits of "context" have to be tested in terms of scale, and the potential of multiple contexts to coexist within the same architectural design problem must be investigated. From the very limited sense of the site, to the urban and regional parameters, the architect is faced with the challenge of establishing contextual definitions to increase the complexity of his or her response.

005 : kelleher house

The task that I have tried to outline above is not a clear-cut phase of the design process for Axi:Ome. **Analysis is not regarded simply as a pre-meditative component in the design process that exists as a phase, which gives way to a somewhat heuristic solution.** Each and every project is handled within different analytical

[iv] Oxford English Dictionary, 2nd Online Edition, 2001. <http://dictionary.oed.com>.

on Axi:Ome llc's trajectory:

contextualizing program, programming context

processes. It is with the analytical diagramming that design starts to emerge and during which possibilities of programming are explored. A dialogue between context and program leads to the redefinition of both, and a constant analysis of this interaction shapes the design. In other words, **the programmatic brief gets contextualized through its inevitable rewriting, while the context gets redefined**. Through the help of computer-aided design tools, the unexpected dynamics of the interaction can be efficiently monitored. Volumetric entities are rethought and reconfigured in terms of topography, climatic variables, local typology, or spatial conventions, whereas the definition of a context can be rewritten by the insertion of an unexpected programmatic density or element. Circulation, depending on the problem, can take on the role of generating the volumes, or can be subdued to an interstitial character. By juxtaposing the development of a site in history on the same representational plane, the effaced potentials of a context can be unearthed.

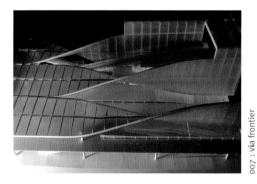

007 : via frontier

008 : book house

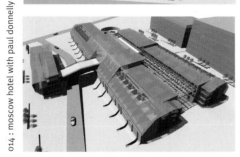

014 : moscow hotel with paul donnelly

In an age of environmental consciousness, such studies need not be limited to the built realm, and can actually point to the potentials of the modified natural environment by reversing some of the processes that led to its transformation. Digital media can enrich today's design practice by cutting-edge production hardware that translates the digital into the material, but the easy transference also threatens to impoverish architectural quality by severing the links between structure and space. By privileging the skin, such disconnection may lead the designer to overlook the contribution of structure to space and drop one aesthetic component of the architectural result. One of Axi:Ome's strong interests is to keep the relationship between the digital model and the material model under constant check by building several constructional models. These models follow the digital models in numerous scales in order to check the relationship of structure to space, and to explore the material possibilities of complex building forms that digital media helps to create. In "The Book House," conjoining programmatic entities that provided the initial mass were digitally analyzed. Following the analysis, a physical model that explored the possibilities of timber lamination was built to investigate the spatial qualities that emerged from the dialogue between structure, program, and in this example, cladding. This process

contextualizing program, programming context

usually allows the generation of constructional analogies. In the end the process pointed to possibilities of employing boat construction techniques. A similar process took place in the design of "Via Frontier," and a composite steel and plastic structure was designed to carry the multimedia screens that folded and spanned 150 feet.

In order to be able to meet the demands of its design policies, **Axi:Ome is configured as an interdisciplinary practice and as an experimental studio**. It exists as a platform to exploit the usually conflicting tendencies of the academic and the practical aspects of the discipline, and aims to transform the prevalent office organization. By being heavily involved in architecture and urban design research, and the development of multimedia, it attempts to enrich the organization of the design office by combining several design disciplines in a melting pot—instead of compartmentalizing their role in the design process. Axi:Ome explores the possible productive outcomes of these disciplines by giving them equal footing in the design process, the effects of which aim to be undistinguishable in the product. Conventional design practices within a discipline are sought metaphorical applications within the other. A building can spring into life out of a graphic or the hyper textual structure of a multimedia product or vice versa. The organizing principles of an astronaut's space wear can be reinterpreted as the climatic interface of a suburban house.

Axi:Ome develops its strength from the will to challenge these issues altogether in the numerous problems presented in this book. Its trajectory is clear in a world that seems to change faster and more dramatically than ever, with it changing our notions of architecture.

lynnette widder

Axi:Ome

the logics of repetition

We all know by now—or have been told—that tectonics is square and blobs are groovy.[i] The point is well taken in regard to certain questions: why should architects be beholden to a theory that was intended to account in the 19th century for the disruptions to the traditional ethics of the building arts by the then-new technology?[ii] The ease with which machines could work all materials, the lack of physical resistance (and its concomitant logical limitations) to the will of the designer, the implications of separating bearing from space-defining elements, the irrefutable need for and ability to construct very large repetitively-structured buildings—these are all the subtext of the early 19th century theories of tectonics, from Bötticher to Semper.[iii] If all these forces were in turn championed by the mid-20th century, then they have become a banal fact by now.[iv]

[i] Greg Lynn, "Blobs (Or Why Tectonics is Square and Topology is Groovy)," *Any* 14, (1996): 58-62. [ii] Kenneth Frampton, "Industrialization and the Crises in Architecture," in *Oppositions Reader* ed. Michael Hays, (New York: Princeton Architectural Press, 1998): 39-63. There is no coincidence regarding the political overtones of Frampton's argument and his citing of Semper, who was part of the same exile German intellectual circle as Karl Marx. [iii] This is the argument I make in an unpublished lecture, given at a symposium on Jean Prouve, on April 12, 2002 at Columbia University and at Cranbrook Academy in April 2001. [iv] I am thinking particularly of the work of such architects/builders as Konrad Wachsmann and Jean Prouve, who designed both processes of fabrication—wood in Wachsmann's case and metal in Prouve's—as well as their products.

Nevertheless, the two central repercussions of this outdated debate—the primacy of means of production over material and the logic of repetition —are obviously present in the repercussions of digital technologies within architecture. Axi:Ome's work specifically and as part of a larger moment, describes this transposition, from industrial to digital "revolutions."

001 : parallel church

At the same time, the work represents another, futurist position. It celebrates transformations in the field of spatial communication. Its use of digital media aspires to creating an armature for habitation, which can account for both ephemeral motion and the staging of spontaneous performance, or everyday life. By creating a spatial boundary that is developed, that resists understanding from a single, static viewpoint, this architecture references space as continually unfolding "practice."[v]

004 : sandol church

The spaces and figures at stake are sinuous, seamless and isotropic. They are inseparable from the technology, which helped to derive them, which described them and which, ultimately, will produce them as habitable constructs. Each project traces the movements and moments of occupation, which will occur within them. Each also takes into account the fact that, whatever its larger-scale qualities, it will be made of pieces. The seamlessness of unfolding space is married to the expression of component parts. This is not a concession to "build-ability." It is an acknowledgement of how this particular digital technology operates at the moment of production. It is the point at which "tectonics" moves from the 19th century into the present.

005 : kelleher house

The Parallel Church is conceived as a series of lines contiguous with the contours of the ground: its walls are constructed of a series of parallel horizontal strips. In the Sandol Church, the construction of a wall from serial lines or strips is pushed further: the lines agglomerate to define building

[v] The terms of the argument are based, at least initially, on such texts as Michel DeCerteau's *The Practice of Everyday Life* and have spawned an entire vocabulary for discussing the potentials of digitally-based architecture.

portions, each of which has its own particular orientation of line. Contiguous space is made subject to the traces of the rapid prototyping machine, which in turn become associated with the same process of fabrication at another scale in another material. By the same token, contiguous space is subjected to another partitioning, the serial sections which the architect still needs to study and refine—and will ultimately reconstitute itself in the "practiced" experience.

The Kelleher House is encompassed by an absolutely contiguous surface, again indexed by inscribed lines despite the painstaking repression of "structure." In the Jaguar Dealership, the ramps themselves—the contiguous surfaces that define the building—are projected onto the exterior skin in an analogous use of line.

Most difficult is the idea that repetition has any place at all in this genre of digitally produced—and therefore infinitely variable—building. Each of the lines drawn differs from all the others. These differences compound themselves until the developed surface is defined. Regardless of its genesis, the developed surface is, however, still ruled, partitioned. Repetition is legible in the increment of each section or each enclosing member. The ruled surface is at the center of the incredibly difficult art of descriptive geometry, ostensibly made obsolete by the capacity for digital data to move from representational to production arenas. The still-present need for dissection—for the purpose of the author's understanding of his work or the workman's mounting of it—indicates its last and un-usurpable area of relevance: in the definition of those vital lines' position, trajectory, orientation.

001

PARALLEL CHURCH

DESIGN PRINCIPALS
sung ho kim with jung hyun hwang

PROJECT COORDINATORS
jeffrey yan
roger bechtiger

DESIGN TEAM
brandon petrella
christopher alonso
egils ramans
hedieh woigani
lina sergie
mara noble
sehzat oner

RANGSIT:THAILAND

Axi:Ome | digital models

view toward the entry ramps

view toward the minister's house

physical model

view toward sermon spaces

floor plans

Axi:Ome

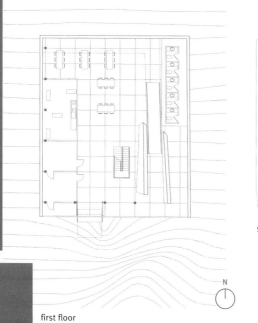

first floor

N

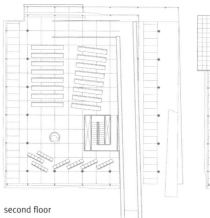

second floor

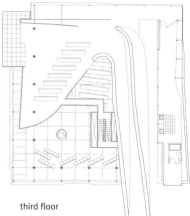

third floor

The Parallel Church attempts to articulate the spatial configuration of a sacred space (Mircea Eliade's definition: space between earth and heaven). Rosalind Krauss's and Yve-Alain Bois's "A User's Guide to Entropy" operated as the model for the investigation in the project. The idea of entropy challenges the existing notion of the value of materiality, the transformation of scale, the informing of existing inactive structures becoming the forms in question.

Utilizing the vertical sections, the church transforms the space between two visually permeable surfaces. The interstitial space continues into the sequence of the entry corridor, a catacomb chamber, integrating the landscape with the building. The vertical corridor walls fold into and through the horizontal slabs of the upper sermon floors, allowing a continuous material pulsation throughout the space. The construction of the entry corridor defines the sacred space, a bridge between earth and heaven, a place that the viewer's visual logic and body cannot occupy. The beholder experiences a structural blindness (Rosalind Krauss's definition of Robert Smithson's work: Enantiomorphic Chamber), a space of ricocheting light, a cross firing of reflections, and unsynthesizable vanishing points in the entry corridor.

fourth floor

The programs distribute on both sides of the entry corridor, allocating an accumulation of densities to frame the lightness of the internal space. The interaction between the public and private spaces facilitates a social flow to the building. The minister's house and the church integrate through the interfacing surfaces that weave distinctive programmatic elements. The ground level contains the submerged subsidiary church programs, under lit to produce an effect of illuminating buoyancy.

view toward light diffuser

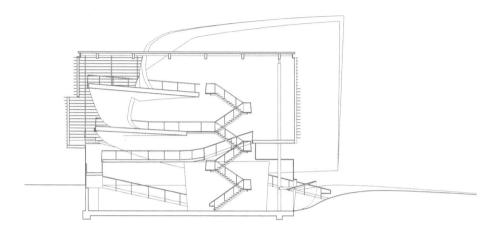

longitudinal section

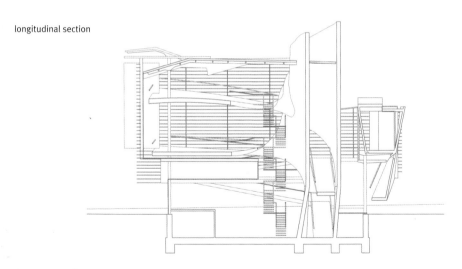

transverse section

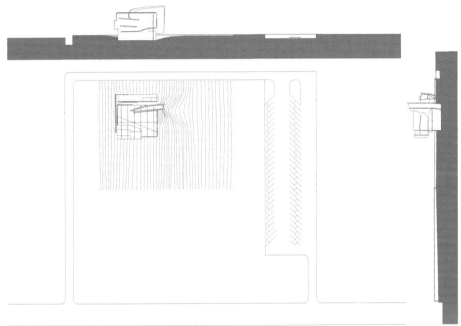

site plan

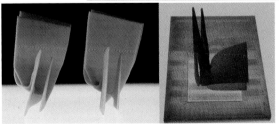

rapid prototype models of parallel surfaces

sectional laminate model of parallel surfaces

The valley of the Tanshui River was once home to rice and vegetable farmers.

TAIPEI:TAIWAN

DESIGN PRINCIPALS
sung ho kim with bryant yeh
DESIGN TEAM
lina sergie

002

Today it is the site of Taipei, the most densely populated territory in Taiwan

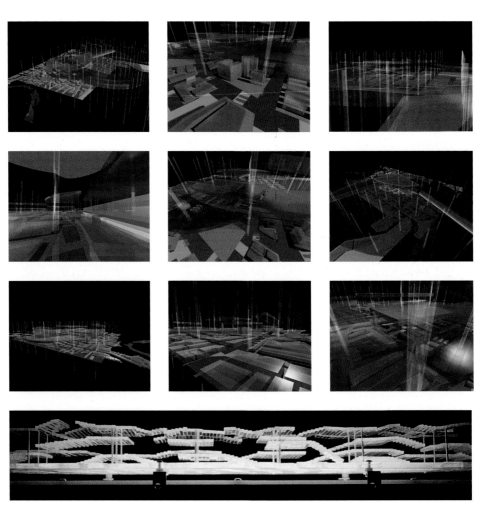

Axi:Ome site models

dense city activity layering (ecological, agricultural, industrial)

sectional zones

The valley of the Tanshui River was once home to rice and vegetable farmers. Today it is the site of Taipei, the most densely populated territory in Taiwan, and the fast-paced center of commerce, government and culture. The population increase is due primarily to an influx of people who are attracted to the city because of its economic and educational opportunities and come from other sectors of the island. This has driven the cost of land to astronomical levels, making Taipei an expensive place to live and work. The high price of housing and office space is forcing the government and many companies to relocate its educational and industrial facilities toward the outskirt territories by decentralizing the city. Taipei's history and identity are engendered by contemporary conditions. As a remnant of an earlier upheaval between Nationalist and Communist factions of Mainland China, Taipei and Taiwan are at the center of crossroads accelerating the development employed by money, zoning, and laissez-faire capitalism.

programmatic layering

Taipei Master Plan is a new city intensified by beautiful patchwork levels, layers, colors, energy, sound and events interweaving into dense stratifications. Taipei is to take its place among the contemporary capital nation-states that exist to facilitate the flow of money, market share and information. The experiments and research of urban strategies deploying

alternative ground formation deepens the urban field, allowing gaps/voids to graft abstract topological grounds by inventing new sectional spaces. The sectional design integrates the public activities, built program masses and landscape systems, to intensify the multiple urban surfaces. The sectional design revolved around long-term planning that begins to unfold new functional garden spaces over time. Green zones in forms of gardens, agricultural networks and centralized park spaces retake the city's old grid by integrating the natural with the modern. Through this process, in-between spaces are generated to do away with the territories of the city, allowing a creation of 'slow' solid spaces that contrast with the modern conditions of speed and fast capital.

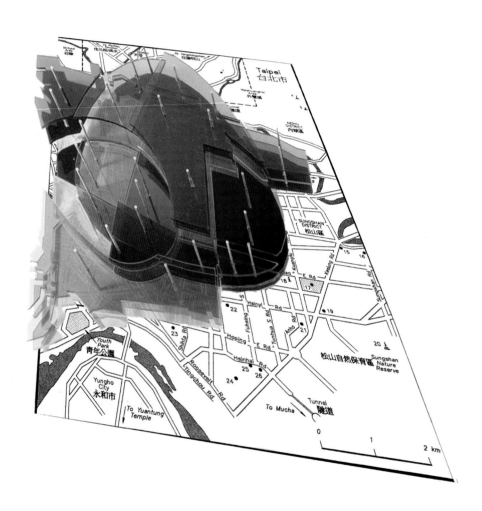

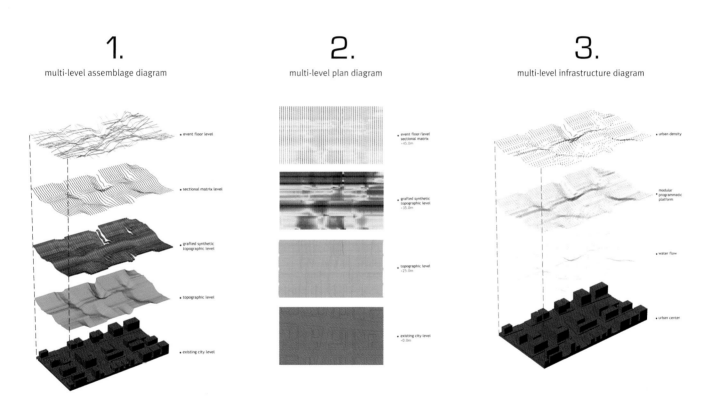

1.
multi-level assemblage diagram

2.
multi-level plan diagram

3.
multi-level infrastructure diagram

- event floor level
- sectional matrix level
- grafted synthetic topographic level
- topographic level
- existing city level

- event floor / level sectional matrix
  +45.0m
- grafted synthetic topographic level
  +35.0m
- topographic level
  +25.0m
- existing city level
  +0.0m

- urban density
- modular programmatic platform
- water flow
- urban center

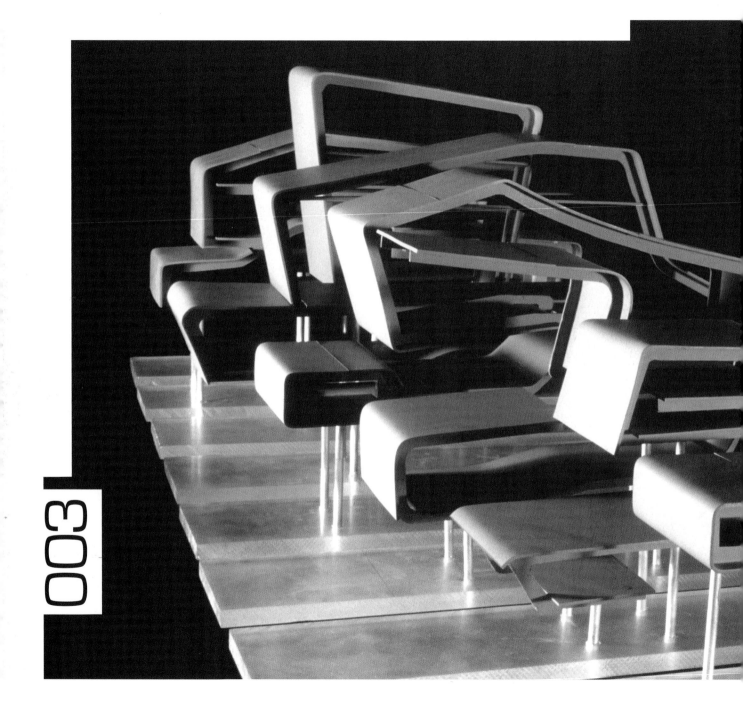

003

OPERA HOUSE

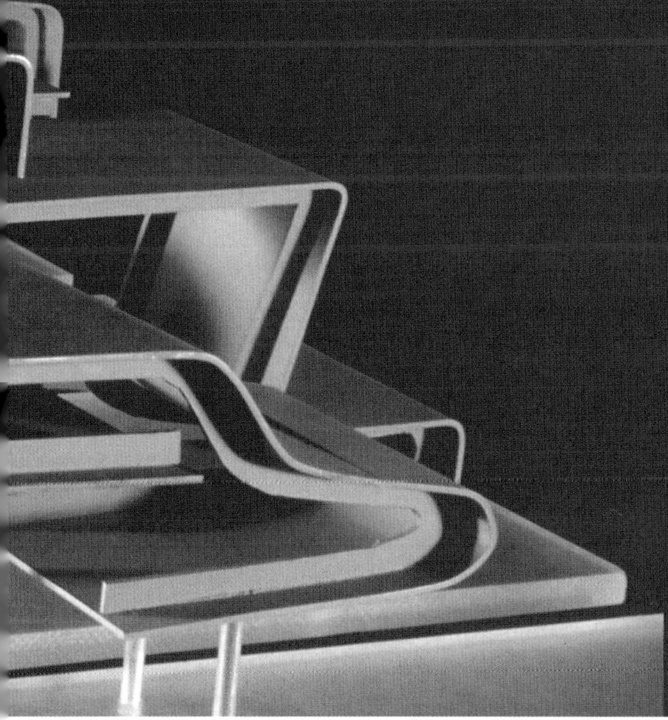

DESIGN PRINCIPALS
sung ho kim with
margot krasso-krasojevic

PROJECT COORDINATORS
roger bechtiger
sehzat oner

DESIGN TEAM
brandon petrella
molly gleason

OSLO:NORWAY

site model

The Opera House research forms a multiple strain of Mobïus wraps that allow open programming and deep planning to activate the harbor site condition in Oslo, Norway. A Mobïus wrap operates through one surface intertwining and folding itself, but in the Opera House there are two dynamic strains of Mobïus wraps, one public and one private. When the two integrate it creates a third condition of open programming of unstable events and activities of operatic programming. This transformative program activates a hybrid condition between public performance and private production, where students and the community can take part in the performing cultural events. Opera House exposes the spatial borders of hidden territories between spectator and spectacle.

The Opera House is organized like a horizontal street with opera programs plugged in, creating a multi-level operatic vertical city. There is a small theater for experimental performances with media screens and the larger theater is a more formal hall with a stage. The building is part of a pier on the site, hovering above the water, allowing it to be an island of theater culture and outdoor performances. The axes of the theaters allocate according to the opening of the stages toward the city. These exposed sections allow the city to open to the performing theater events and unfold the events into the urban landscape. The design strategy of these articulating open sections transforms the differentiated programs to overlap one another in the deep planning process.

Axi:Ome

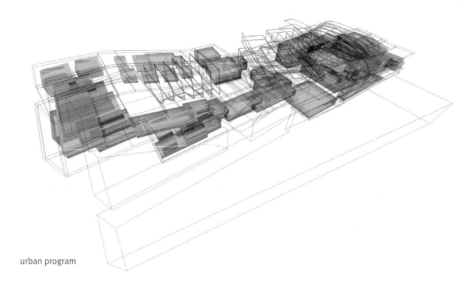

urban program

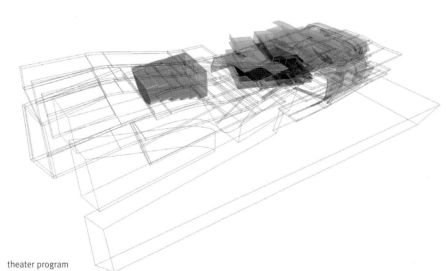

theater program

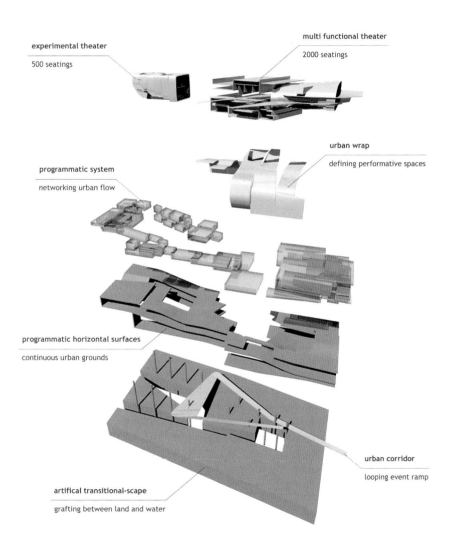

experimental theater

500 seatings

multi functional theater

2000 seatings

urban wrap

defining performative spaces

programmatic system

networking urban flow

programmatic horizontal surfaces

continuous urban grounds

urban corridor

looping event ramp

artifical transitional-scape

grafting between land and water

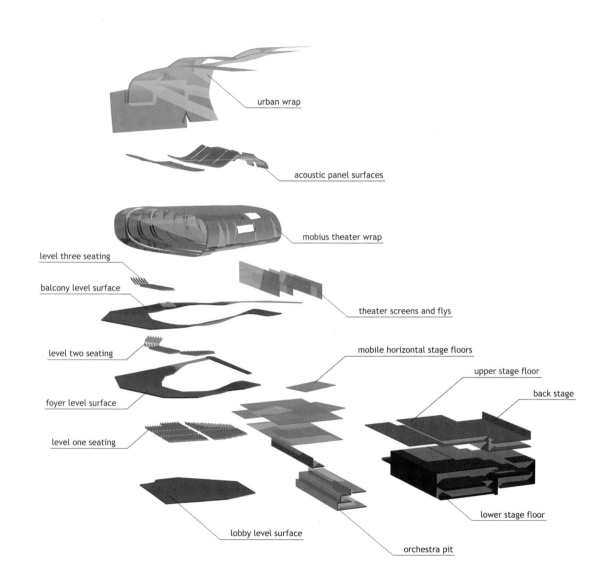

urban wrap

acoustic panel surfaces

mobius theater wrap

level three seating

balcony level surface

theater screens and flys

level two seating

mobile horizontal stage floors

upper stage floor

back stage

foyer level surface

level one seating

lower stage floor

lobby level surface

orchestra pit

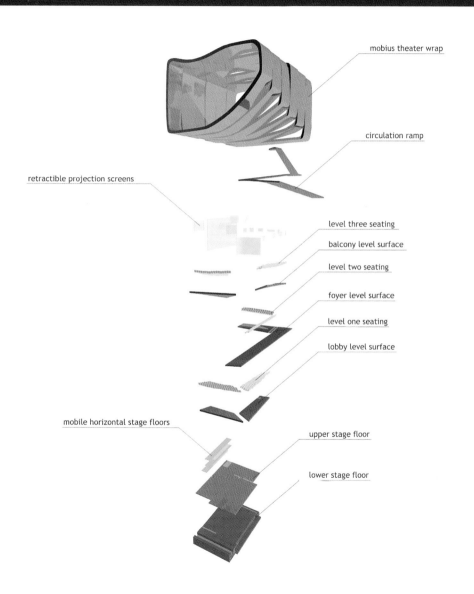

mobius theater wrap

circulation ramp

retractible projection screens

level three seating

balcony level surface

level two seating

foyer level surface

level one seating

lobby level surface

mobile horizontal stage floors

upper stage floor

lower stage floor

DESIGN PRINCIPAL
sung ho kim

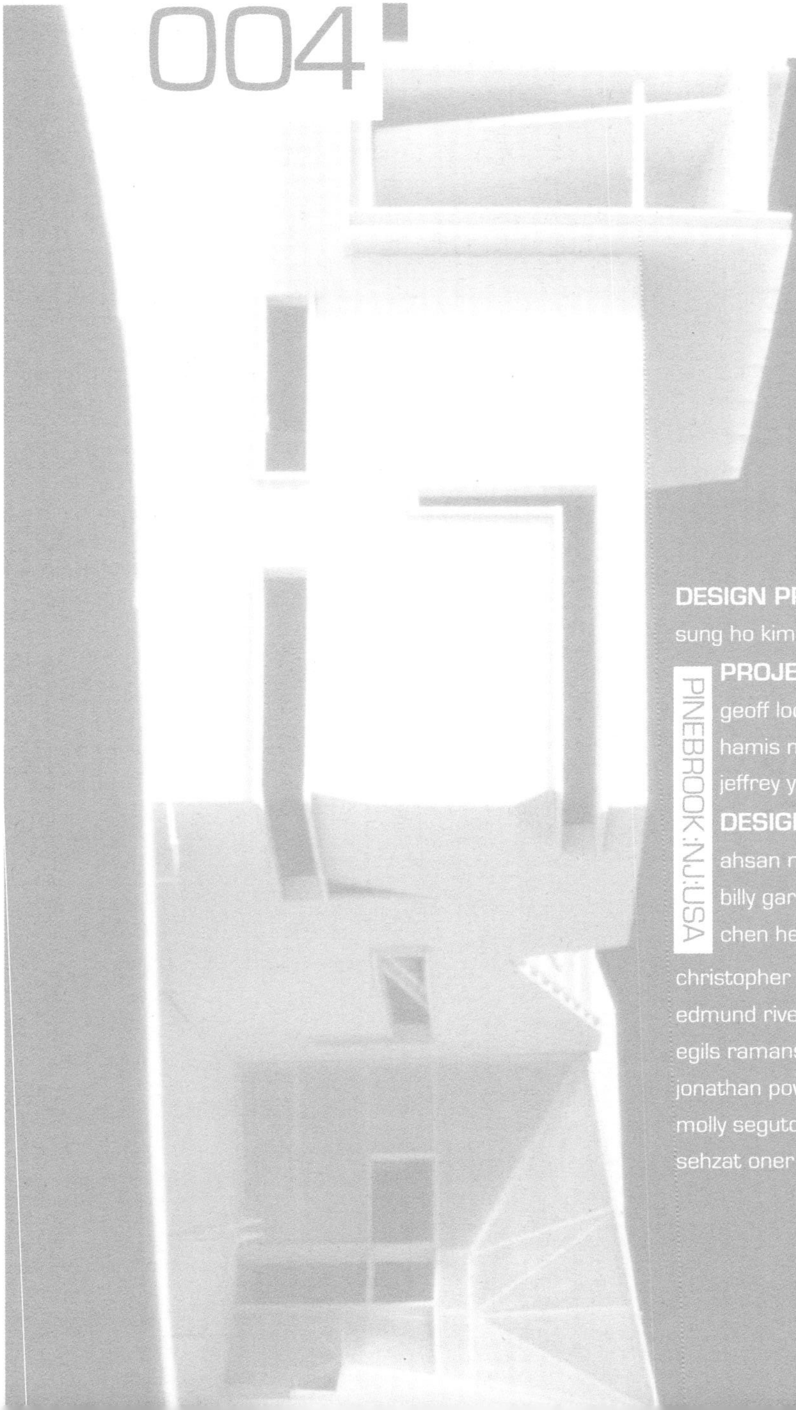

PROJECT COORDINATORS
geoff loo
harris mhando
jeffrey yan

DESIGN TEAM
ahsan najmi
billy garcia
chen he guan
christopher rountos
edmund rivera
egils ramans
jonathan powell
molly seguto
sehzat oner

PINEBROOK :NJ:USA

SANDOL CHURCH

Sandol Church defines a form of architecture that is open to the community. It features a configuration of overlapped and distributed surfaces and programs that are multi-purpose. The unfolding spaces wrap around the existing sacred space, creating a secondary skin of event space. This event space gives the opportunity for a mainly marginalized community to gather, socialize and interact. The extension provides and encourages this interaction and forms the transitory space. The walls of the outside infrastructure morph to embrace the building and form into the undulating roof that encloses the children's space and floating playground.

The sound of children at play and wind flowing through the glass mingles with the echoes of prayer and celebration, thus defining for a moment, a whole in midst of the fragments—the role of a contemporary church in suburban life.

Through the superimposition of architectonic layers the structure unfolds as an open tectonic field. The form of the building dissolves as the structure multiplies into a series of surfaces. The landscape and densely built fabric are interlaced within the network of ramps creating a new assembly of programs and situations.

The design strategy has unified the image of the existing terrain, despite the inherent differences among the fragments. One perceives the infrastructure (freeways and power lines) and suburban fabric (single-family homes and shopping centers) with the landscape as one system. They are the sediments of one and the same geology. This landscape is always subjugated to a process of transformation in which disparate elements conjoin into a fluid spatial continuum. Through mutations and transformations, new morphologies provide the possibility of an architecture of landscape and infrastructure.

Digital diagrams free the preconceived organization of the architecture to form a conceptual framework. The physical models transfer the conceptual to a tectonic framework. Through making, one invents techniques of manipulating the material organization for an emerging material tactility. This allows for a more fluid relationship between parts of the whole. Every condition is conceived as a modulated form where one part affects the rest—the models acting as a tool for the imagination and spatial investigation. The digital diagrams operate within the world of illusions and freedom, while the physical operations become the communicative tool for the design team to focus on spatial interest. In this case, the diagrams elicit the playfulness of the children who inhabit 70 percent of the architecture. They maneuver within various fields on the site, while the adults and automobiles operate with restricted movements. The diagrams also expand the nature of growth in the community. As Korean immigrants are often secluded, they use the church primarily as a communal space for meeting friends and keeping their heritage/culture alive—making the interface of the church and community programs a necessity. By folding and surfacing the landscape and building, the strategy becomes part landscape and part building. The process models allow detail, surface and skin elements to invent the whole.

physical model

wall-skin and playground

physical models

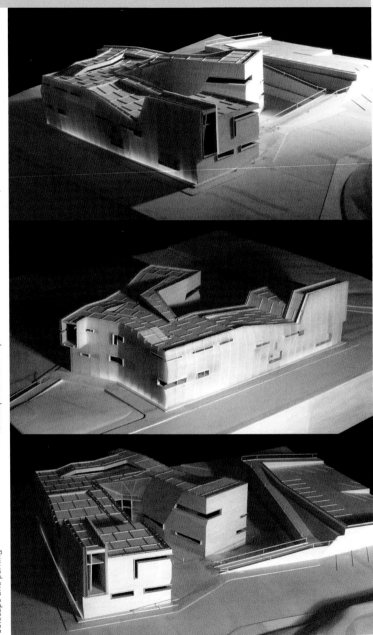

roofscape and wall-skin

roofscape and landscape

roofscape and parking

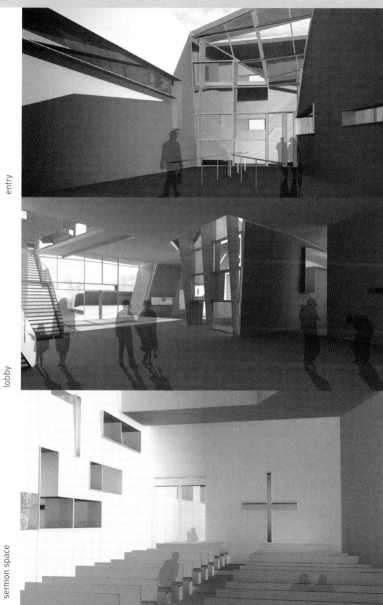

entry

lobby

sermon space

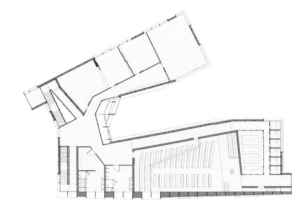

second floor

first floor

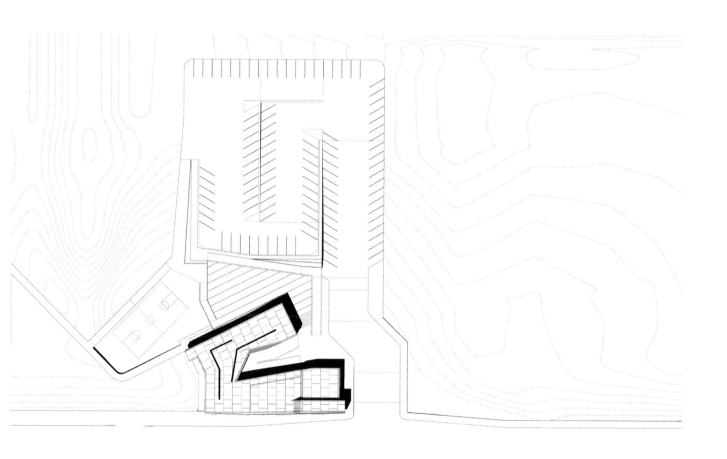

transverse sections

Axi:Ome

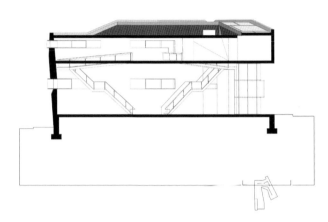

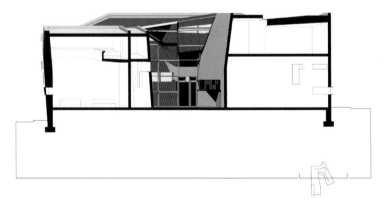

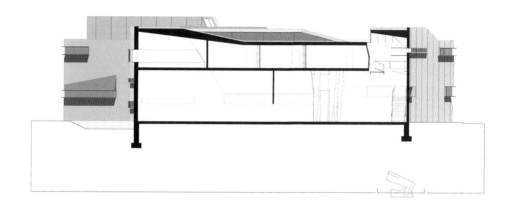

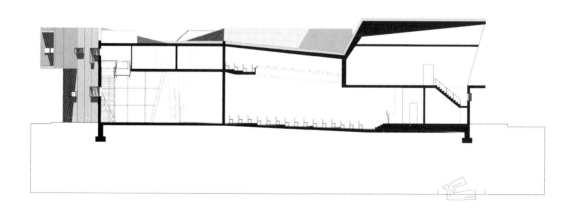

Axi:Ome   territorial strategy diagrams

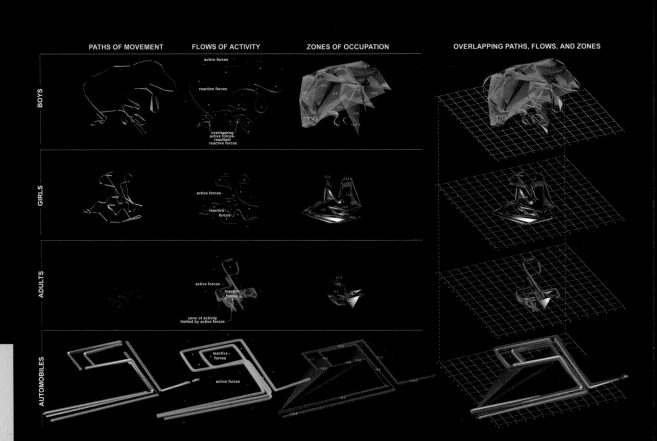

PATHS OF MOVEMENT   FLOWS OF ACTIVITY   ZONES OF OCCUPATION   OVERLAPPING PATHS, FLOWS, AND ZONES

BOYS

active forces

reactive forces

overlapping
active forces-
resultant
reactive forces

GIRLS

active forces

reactive
forces

ADULTS

active forces

reactive
forces

zone of activity
limited by active forces

AUTOMOBILES

reactive
forces

active forces

wall formations

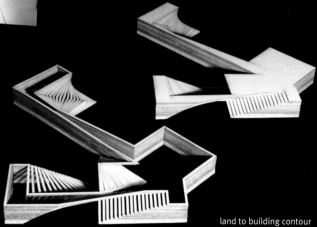

land to building contour

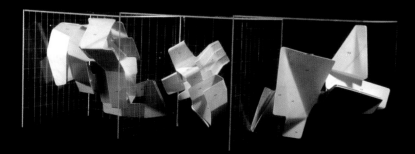

programmatic organization model

005

WEYMOUTH:MA:USA

DESIGN PRINCIPAL
sung ho kim
PROJECT COORDINATOR
jeffrey yan
DESIGN TEAM
abeer seikaly
egils ramans
roger bechtiger
sehzat oner

KELLEHER HOUSE

Axi:Ome

physical models

night view

day view

perforated stainless steel wall/skin

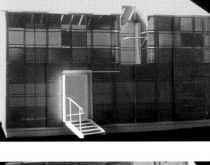

wall/skin: depth, transparency, pattern, and movement

detail of wall/skin

view toward the family room

The Kelleher House is an experiment in redefining the visual, social and spatial relationship of the suburban interface. The project proposes new surfaces and facades onto an existing suburban, New England house. The sectional line diagrams illustrate the complex visual and social networking of the site. The new surfaces reflect this spatial order through animating dynamic facades that change in depth, transparency, pattern and movement. This project is a machine that reorganizes the static environment into a transformative situation.

The design of the astronaut's suit layers creates a protective artificial skin capable of adapting to the surrounding environment. The layers of the exterior wall/skin in the Kelleher House also act as mediators of view, temperature and sound. The water tube system of the insulating layer acts as a natural cooling/heating device in the different seasons depending on the temperature of the fluids pumped through. This enclosure forms the skin that becomes an experiential surface sensitive to texture, light, sound and view, extending the human senses to the boundary of the home. The protective artificial skin, once a suit, now fluctuates into a living space.

woven liquid insulation system

Axi:Ome

with frame

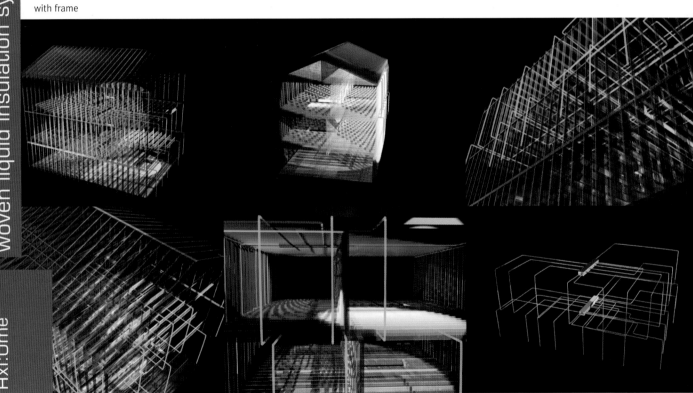

without frame

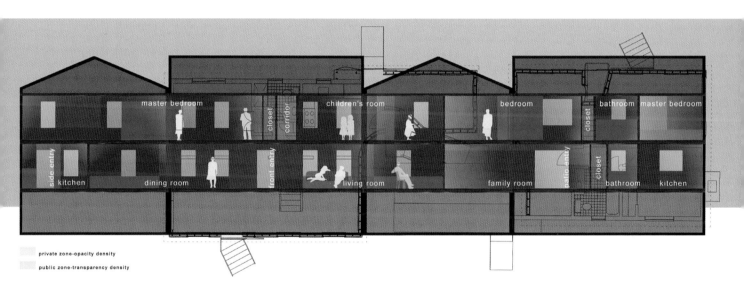

master bedroom — closet — corridor — children's room — bedroom — bathroom — master bedroom

side entry — kitchen — dining room — front entry — living room — family room — patio entry — closet — bathroom — kitchen

private zone-opacity density
public zone-transparency density

006

ALEPPO:SYRIA

DESIGN PRINCIPAL
sung ho kim

PROJECT COORDINATORS
jeffrey yan
lina sergie

DESIGN TEAM
ahsan najmi
egils ramans
jin kwon kim

JAGUAR DEALERSHIP

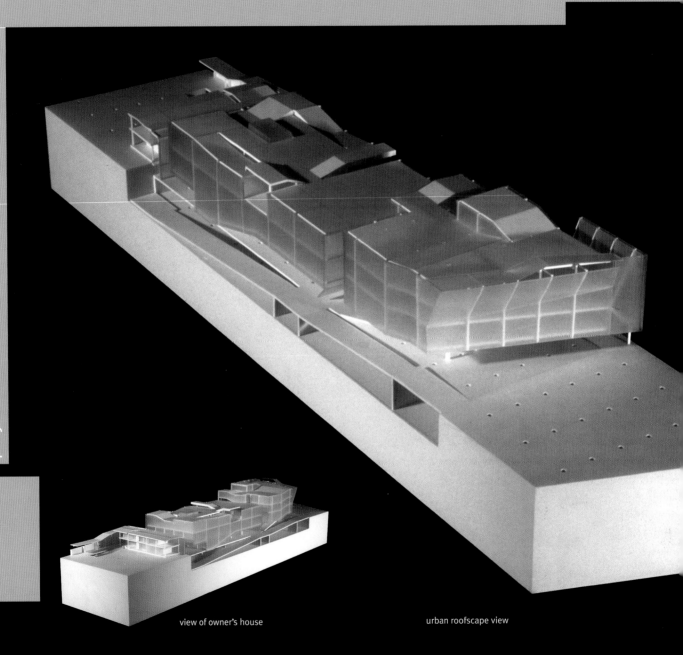

physical models

Axi:Ome

view of owner's house

urban roofscape view

The Jaguar Dealership assembles around the voyeuristic experience of the automobile as a spectacular infrastructural, yet tactile event. This event engages the consumer within a wide range of scales and interests. The client receives and services the car, while the visitors of the dealership act as active spectators to this event. The architecture establishes a new relationship to its context from that of the other structures on the site; because the dealership sits as a gateway to Aleppo, Syria, in the desert prior to the city entrance, the building acts as a mirage connecting itself to the infrastructure of highway, power lines and signage. The spatial conception of the Jaguar Dealership encompasses a multiplicity of events and programs within a complex, yet coherent whole. Movement and change inform the very organization of space itself. The scale and complexity of these buildings move beyond conventional thresholds—as a structure too large to call a "building," it incorporates movement systems and infrastructure as an inherent part of its organization. The Jaguar Dealership engages the extensive program requirements not simply as a building solution, but rather as architecture of dynamic environments.

Axi:Ome

physical models

jaguar dealership façade

multiple layering of infrastructure

dealership and service area

roofscape and yard of owner's house

entry corridor of owner's house

swimming pool and yard
of owner's house

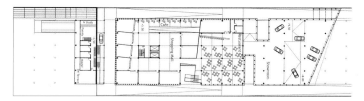

level 3

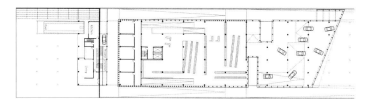

level 2

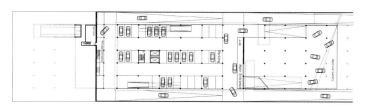

level 1

level 0

strategy diagrams

Axi:Ome

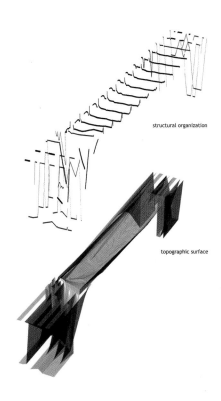

structural organization

topographic surface

disassembled components

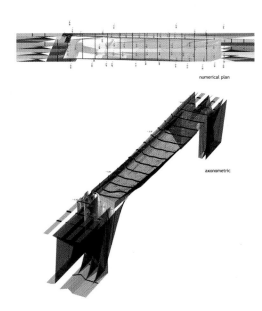

numerical plan

axonometric

abstract topographical conditions

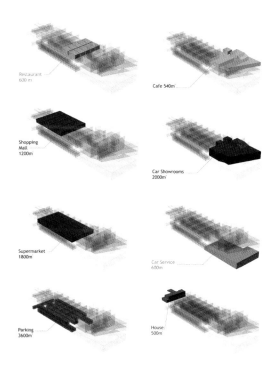

Restaurant
600 m²

Cafe 540m²

Shopping
Mall
1200m²

Car Showrooms
2000m²

Supermarket
1800m²

Car Service
600m²

Parking
3600m²

House
500m²

program areas

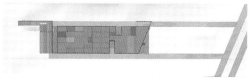

Program Wrapper
Conceptual DeMaterialized wall

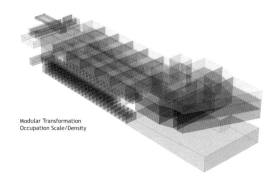

Modular Transformation
Occupation Scale/Density

programmatic zoning

007

VIA FRONTIER

DESIGN PRINCIPALS
sung ho kim with via frontier
development corporation

PROJECT COORDINATORS
hamis mhando
jeffrey yan
jihoon kim

DESIGN TEAM
adni isakovic
ahsan najmi
almin prsic
brandon petrella
christopher rountos
egils ramans
george yam
lincoln lewis
mara noble
mark stenson
michael hahn
paul yam
steven sanderson

DALY CITY:CA:USA

Project: 160,000 square feet of retail and entertainment
Gallery (new product displays)
Free Zone (internet access)
Media Surfaces
Stage

Retail: Hardware
Software
Peripherals
Telecommunications

Internet: ISPs
Travel
Auctions
Finance
Books
Cars
Clothing
Entertainment

Gaming Center: Consoles
Games
Accessories

Computer Education Centers

Mail Services

Specialty Foods

Cinema: Digital Cineplex and Imax

Banking Services

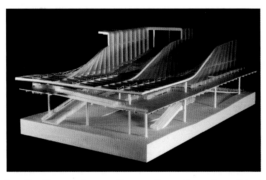

Via Frontier is an innovative hybridization of the typical 'brick and mortar' outlet and 'direct mail' online business. This technological hub is an ultimate venue for direct vendors (those currently without distributorship) to showcase products and services directly to consumers. Existing vendors need to creatively and strategically present ideas and products in parallel with the shifting and emerging technologies. A collective center continuously on the edge of technology, the Via Frontier invites curious consumers with different levels of technological knowledge to interface and experience the latest in the world of media, information, and technology.

Via Frontier is a new form of spatial organization for high technological and commercial space challenging the contemporary system of consumerism. The design strategy develops through the research for 'programmatic transparency,' an operation that shifts from defining formal suburban mall typology, to more flexible organization of consumer information and media. This transformative design process allows for a perpetual dynamic marketplace. Via Frontier is a project that opportunistically develops spatial formations through defining ephemeral compositions of 'form' and 'space.'

media surface model

media catwalk

internet cafe

fiber-optic parking view 1

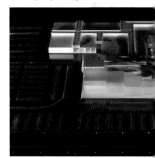

storefront view

view 2

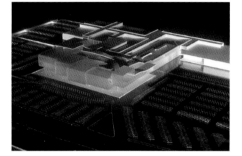

view 3

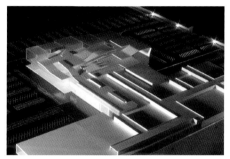

view 4

activated media surface

music media pod

imax theater

longitudinal sectional view

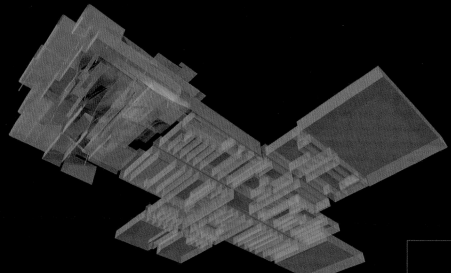

worm's eye view

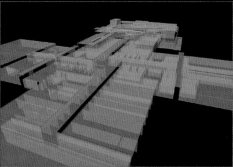

modularity of site model

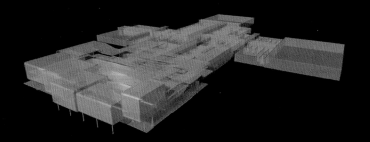

roofscape view

008

BOOK HOUSE

DESIGN PRINCIPALS
sung ho kim with stuart steck
PROJECT COORDINATORS
brandon petrella
geoff loo
DESIGN TEAM
adni isakovic
ahsan najmi
almin prsic
kenichi sato
lincoln lewis
michael hahn
nick taylor

NARRAGANSETT:RI:USA

The Book House develops through spatial and programmatic mapping processes that allows for continuous and smooth event surfaces. These bifurcated surfaces define the vectoring of movement and the logic of optimization of the connections between spaces and programs. The surfaces fold literally, creating non-hierarchical ambiguities between spaces and forms of fluid nature. The various recognizable events occur on the continuity of the surfaces by folding up according to the contours and fluctuations of movements. Program selections emphasize the surface plays that they implement: to bend, to warp—surfaces morph successively to a wall, a floor and a terrace—always in a state of becoming another condition. Oscillating between the translucent surfaces, technically autonomous and geological, or organic continuity, the Book House questions its limits. Between disappearance and event, the architecture explores a space in transition.

The Book House generates through the territorial occupation of the binary form and its possible programmatic conditions. The house operates as a continuous surface and a space for work and leisure. The binary form is the main circuit for infrastructural flows, movements, programs and spatial organizations.

stuart steck

Axi:Ome

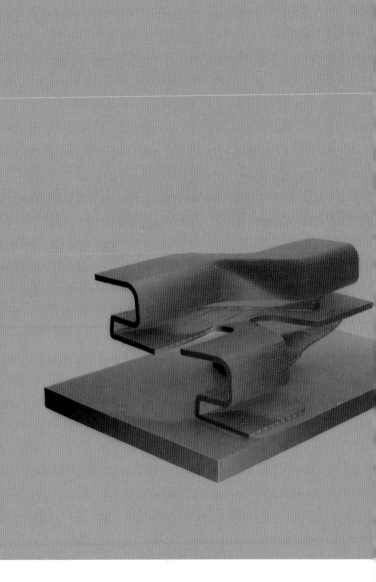

Phase I: The Birth of a Project

Five years ago, I asked Sung Ho Kim to design a house for me. At the time, we were both graduate students—Sung Ho at MIT, myself at Boston University—and neither of us had the resources to finance such an ambitious project; like most graduate students, we barely had enough money to cover our monthly expenses—let alone build a house. Nevertheless, despite the financial obstacles that stood in our path, we decided that the benefits of collaborating together would far outweigh any hardships we might suffer down the road. Indeed, as far as we were concerned, this project offered us an opportunity to enter into a critical dialogue outside the institutional framework of academia. But more importantly, it offered us the chance to combine theory and practice: a chance not only to articulate our own ideas about architecture and design, but to test these ideas against the conventional limits of architectural practice. In any case, we had nothing to lose by trying.

Given our financial constraints, Sung Ho and I started the project with relatively modest expectations. After discussing various options and alternatives, we agreed that the house should fulfill two simple criteria: one formal and one functional. In formal terms, the structure was intended to convey a sense of openness and transparency.[i] Ideally, this would be achieved by enclosing the interior space within a glass and steel box—a strategy that sprang from our mutual interest in mid-century design (such as Philip Johnson's Glass House). In functional terms, the house was to accommodate my collection of books and journals, while at the same time providing an environment that would be conducive to different forms of intellectual activity and aesthetic

[i] At this stage in the project, Sung Ho and I were primarily interested in creating the effects of "literal" (as opposed to "phenomenal") transparency. For a discussion of these two types of transparency, see Colin Rowe and Robert Slutzky, "Transparency: Literal and Phenomenal", *The Mathematics of the Ideal Villa and Other Essays* (Cambridge: The MIT Press, 1976).

production. That is to say, we wanted to construct a building that would serve as a gathering place for artists and intellectuals—one that would encourage both theoretical discourse and scholarly debate.[ii]

As our careers developed, however, Sung Ho and I came to expect much more from this project and we began to chafe against the formal and functional limitations that we had initially imposed on the house. Indeed, during the course of our collaboration, it not only became apparent that we shared a number of theoretical concerns regarding the "regulatory effects" of modern architecture, but it became clear that the project offered us a unique opportunity to address these issues in both structural and conceptual terms. In turning our attention to the question of how discipline and control are exercised through architecture, Sung Ho and I were deeply influenced by theorists such as Louis Althusser, Michel Foucault and Gilles Deleuze. Based upon their critique of ideology and power, we were eager to interrogate existing systems of architectural discourse and to redefine the ways in which buildings shape our sense of subjectivity.

In this respect, while our initial criteria continued to serve as a general starting point for Sung Ho's design, his final plan for the house evolved into something far more complex and provocative than anything we had originally envisioned. Indeed, rather than simply designing the house as a repository for my books, Sung Ho devised a structure that is intended to transform the nature of architectural experience and our relationship to the world around us. But how, we might ask, will Sung Ho's design accomplish this task? How can this project bring about such far-reaching changes in both our architecture and our culture?

[ii] Sung Ho places an extraordinary degree of emphasis on the role of dialogue and debate within his practice. Rather than acting as a "master builder"—i.e. one who privileges his own creative ego and asserts his authority within the studio—Sung Ho works with a team of young designers, allowing his projects to evolve through a process of open collaboration. Indeed, since I have known him, Sung Ho has developed a series of strategies to suppress his authorial voice. By inviting a plurality of voices to enter into the design process, Sung Ho not only embraces the notion of anti-individualism, but he seeks to produce a body of architecture that opens itself to radically diverse audiences.

In explaining his work, for example, Sung Ho has written, "Roland Barthes implies the birth of the reader coexists with the death of the author. The autobiographical author is present but absent from the work such that the reader becomes collaborator. The reader constitutes the work. The reader, then, is structurally folded into the work. The matrix of the book is formulated by the reader and not only by the author, and hence becomes a collective and social activity."

If buildings function to define our sense of "self" in relation to both physical space and cultural discourse, then the Book House—as it has come to be known—gives rise to a mode of human consciousness that is remarkably fluid and thus resists the imposition of social constraints. Indeed, with its seemingly "formless" interior, the building engenders a new type of cognitive experience, one that challenges the ideals and norms that have governed architectural practice for nearly a century.[iii] In so doing, the Book House promises to liberate us from the yoke of tradition and authority; it not only calls into question accepted ideas about form and function, but it disrupts the mechanisms of power that are enforced through our buildings and institutions.

Yet, the Book House transcends simple notions of opposition and resistance. In keeping with Sung Ho's commitment to rethink the discipline of architecture and to reconsider its role within contemporary culture, this project represents a form of critical practice. As such, it is intended to accomplish four distinct tasks: 1) to challenge traditional assumptions about structure and space; 2) to redefine the social function of architectural practice; 3) to produce new modes of subjectivity and experience; 4) to undermine existing systems of ideology and discourse. As Sung Ho recently explained:

> I understand architecture as a form of research; a complex system of cultural conditions that can capitalize on technological innovations, socio-economic developments, political ideologies, and cultural tendencies. Architecture, formally a discipline opposing new ideas, needs to embrace the new in order to remain valid in contemporary society. It must facilitate permutations within the context of everyday life by searching for the potential of new patterns of cultural productions.[iv]

[iii] In our discussions concerning this project, both Sung Ho and I were drawn to the concept of "formlessness," particularly as it has been theorized by Yve-Alain Bois and Rosalind Krauss. According to Bois and Krauss, the notion of "formlessness"—which first appeared in the writings of Georges Bataille during the 1920s—has a specific "use value": it is intended to serve a deconstructive purpose. In this respect, "formless" is not simply an adjective that describes a particular state of being, but is an operation that actively displaces and/or collapses traditional categories of "form" and "content." In their own work, for example, Bois and Krauss employ the operation of *l'informe* in order to subvert the aesthetic claims of high modernism and to challenge its underlying principles of formal purity, artistic autonomy and spiritual transcendence. See Yve-Alain Bois and Rosalind Krauss, *Formless: A User's Guide* (New York: Zone Books, 1997): 21. [iv] Sung Ho Kim, conversation with the author, 7 February 2002.

Phase II: Disrupting Dominant Modes of Power and Control

Although its coercive force often goes unmarked by the general public, modern architecture serves as an instrument of power and control.[v] Indeed, whether we realize it or not, buildings impose both order and discipline upon our lives; they not only establish a fixed hierarchy of structure and meaning within our built environment, but they regulate our actions and experiences as well. Hence, even when architects strive to produce the effect of open, volumetric space—as in the work of Mies van der Rohe—their buildings dictate specific patterns of movement and behavior, forcing us to perform prescribed tasks and rituals as we move from one architectural coordinate to another.[vi]

As Michel Foucault has argued in his analysis of the "panopticon," this system of power and control operates in a particularly efficient manner; it conditions us to act as the agents of our own oppression.[vii] In other words, through a constant process of regulation, we gradually internalize different modes of subjectivity and power, learning to govern our actions and behaviors without consciously doing so. As each individual assumes responsibility for his or her own subjugation, the unspoken threat of punishment is enough to guarantee our continued obedience. In fact, once we are fully conditioned to behave as self-policing subjects, it is no longer necessary for the state to assert its authority through explicit displays of violence and force. For Foucault, this process of domination comes to permeate every layer of human existence and thus represents the "automatic functioning of power" in its ideal form.

[v] In a short article published in the journal *Documents*, Georges Bataille first called attention to the interrelationship of power and architecture. Writing in 1929, Bataille claimed: "Architecture is the expression of the very soul of society... In fact it is only the ideal soul of society, that which has the authority to command and prohibit that is expressed in architectural compositions, properly speaking. Thus great monuments are erected like dikes, opposing the logic and majesty of authority against all disturbing elements: it is in the form of cathedral or palace that Church or State speaks to the multitudes and imposes silence upon them. It is, in fact, obvious that monuments inspire social prudence and often even real fear." Cited in Denis Hollier, *Against Architecture: The Writings of Georges Bataille*, trans. Betsy Wing (Cambridge: The MIT Press, 1992): 46-47. [vi] Despite its utopian claims, modernist architecture has come to embody certain forms of discursive power. In this regard, my reading of high modernism contrasts sharply with that of K. Michael Hays. In his discussion of modernist architecture, Hays sees critical value in the work of Mies van der Rohe. See K. Michael Hays, "Critical Architecture: Between Culture and Form," *Perspecta* 21 (1984): 14-29. For a discussion of glass architecture and its critical value, I refer readers to Branden Joseph's article entitled "John Cage and the Architecture of Silence," *October* 81 (Summer 1997): 81-104. [vii] Michel Foucault, *Discipline and Punish: The Birth of a Prison*, translated by Alan Sheridan (New York: Pantheon, 1979).

In order to dismantle the authoritative language of modernist architecture, Sung Ho not only rejects conventional notions of "form" and "function," he turns his back on the concepts of structural rationalism and formal closure. Indeed, rather than subdividing the Book House into a network of box-like rooms and functional units, Sung Ho has arranged the interior into a series of fluid spaces and unregulated "zones." Devoid of right angles and straight lines, these internal zones fold into one another without recognizable boundaries, negating the sense of spatial order and structural logic that ordinarily governs architectural experience. Instead of restricting us, the internal structure engenders a state of indeterminacy and flux. From the moment we enter the Book House, the principles of unity and coherence give way to our own (unstable) perceptions—a situation that serves to heighten our awareness of the architectural context and its structural irregularities. As in the music of John Cage, the laws of contingency and chance play a determinative role in our interaction with surrounding environment and thus disrupt the patterns of movement and behavior that are usually imposed upon us.

Given the highly dynamic nature of this space, our relationship with the building is never static or prescribed, but develops in unforeseen ways. Every aspect of the Book House has the capacity to transform itself anew, defying both our habits and expectations. As one circulates through the house, the entire structure seems to oscillate between "form" and "non-form," as if it is undergoing a process of metamorphosis: walls appear to mutate into ceilings; ceilings appear to meld into floors; floors appear to fuse into stairways; stairways appear to morph into bookcases; and bookcases appear to dissolve back into walls. Like the Möbius strip, which continually folds back onto itself in a perpetual loop, the Book House has neither beginning nor end, but greets us with a constant tide of change.[viii]

[viii] In discussing his own work, Sung Ho often points to the Möbius strip as a source of influence. Undoubtedly, Sung Ho's interest in the Möbius strip can be traced back to the Brazilian artist Lygia Clark. Working in the 1960s and 1970s, Clark sought to break away from the formalist claims of high modernism, particularly as they were expressed within the context of geometric abstraction. By using the Möbius strip as a conceptual device, Clark hoped to produce new forms of subjective experience, thus liberating the viewer. In her words, the Möbius strip "breaks with our spatial habits: right/left; front/back, etc. It forces us to experience limitless time and continuous space." Cited in M. Catherine de Zegher, *"Inside the Visible,"* Inside the Visible: An elliptical traverse of 20th century art in, of, and from the feminine (Cambridge: The MIT Press, 1996): 34.

Since there are no fixed signs of structure or meaning to regulate our experiences, the Book House gives rise to an infinite range of activities and events. As Sung Ho has explained, every element within the house is open to a continuous process of definition and redefinition, thereby "creating unexpected programmatic possibilities and spatial effects." Aside from the kitchen and bathrooms, the "function" of each space is contingent upon our movements and behaviors. In contrast to more conventional examples of architecture, the Book House evolves "performatively rather than syntactically." That is to say, the building takes shape in response to the needs and actions of its inhabitants, changing from moment to moment in order to create new surfaces, new spaces and new programs. For people whose lives have been made routine by the hegemonic norms of society, the effects of Sung Ho's work can be rather exhilarating—much like a trip to a carnival.

By privileging the individual as the focal point of his design process, Sung Ho shifts the locus of meaning and power away from the architecture itself. Through our interaction with the Book House, we begin to reclaim sovereignty over our thoughts and experiences. In this sense, Sung Ho's design is intended to produce an effect of emancipation; for it not only awakens our sense of individual consciousness, but it offers us a renewed feeling of freedom and autonomy.[ix] Liberated from the stranglehold of discipline and control, we are once again free to explore different forms of subjectivity and knowledge, and to experience an unmediated state of spontaneity and pleasure.

[ix] In using such disruptive techniques to reawaken our sense of self-awareness, Sung Ho employs a procedure that the Russian formalists called *ostranenie*. The notion of *ostranenie* was first theorized by Victor Shklovsky in his essay "Art as Technique" (1916). According to Shklovsky, the purpose of art is to de-familiarize our sense of perception, which becomes automated or habituated over time. In his words, "the technique of art is to make objects 'unfamiliar,' to make forms difficult, to increase the difficulty and length of perception... Art exists that one may recover the sensation of life; it exists to make one feel things..." Victor Shklovsky, "Art as Technique," *Russian Formalist Essays*, translated by Lee T. Lemon and Marion J. Reis (Lincoln: University of Nebraska Press, 1965): 12.

Phase III. Challenging the Limits of Architectural Practice

In historical terms, Sung Ho joins a long line of artists and architects who have sought to challenge both the formal language and social authority of modernist architecture—a lineage that extends from Frederick Kiesler (who first conceived his Endless House in the 1920s), to Gordon Matta-Clark (who devised the concept of "Anarchitecture" in the 1970s).[X] Yet, while Sung Ho is clearly mindful of the past, his approach to architecture looks towards the future. In particular, he seeks to redefine the ways in which architects approach the task of designing buildings. Indeed, rather than adhering to accepted methods of drafting and design—which are often limited by traditional ideas of form and function—Sung Ho harnesses the power of digital technologies to forge a more fluid and dynamic conception of architectural space.

In the process of designing the Book House, for example, Sung Ho employed different types of electronic media to redefine our understanding of domestic architecture and its relationship to everyday life. In order to accomplish this task he programmed his computer to perform a complex set of operations: first, to calculate the vast range of activities that are common to domestic life; second, to quantify the ways in which individuals occupy their homes in both spatial and temporal terms; third, to produce simulations based upon these computations. Using these simulations as the basis for his design, Sung Ho then developed a series of "virtual" models, enabling him to test different spatial configurations against an almost infinite number of functional possibilities. By allowing him to stretch the boundaries of architectural practice, digital technologies have made it possible for Sung Ho to produce structures that anticipate the contingencies of human existence and that express a spirit of utopian optimism. In this regard, the Book House embodies Sung Ho's desire "to open up a realm of freedom and experience by developing architecture that transcends social, political, and ideological constraints."[xi]

[X] Frederick Kiesler was a member of the European avant-garde, whose work cut across the boundaries of art and architecture. Kiesler's design for the Endless House—which was predicated upon a series of organic forms—came to fruition in the 1950's and reflected the influence of both Surrealism and Dada. For more information regarding Kiesler's work, I refer readers to Lisa Phillips, *Frederick Kiesler* (New York: Whitney Museum of American Art, 1989).

During his short career, Gordon Matta-Clark sought to deconstruct accepted notions of art and architecture—oftentimes by literally disemboweling and/or dissecting buildings. In his words: "By undoing a building there are many aspects of the social conditions against which I am gesturing: first, to open a state of enclosure, which had been preconditioned not only by physical necessity but by the industry that profligates suburban and urban boxes as a context for insuring a passive, isolated consumer—a virtually captive audience... The very nature of my work with buildings takes issue with a functionalist attitude to the extent that this kind of self-righteous vocational responsibility has failed to question, or reexamine, the quality of life being serviced." Cited in Donald Wall, "Gordon Matta-Clark's Building Dissections," *Arts Magazine,* May 1976: 76. xi Sung Ho Kim, email to the author, 9 March.

Axi:Ome

physical models

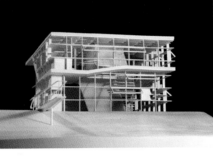

view toward landscape platform

view toward binary form

view toward staircase

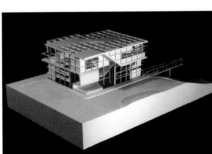

view toward roofscape

view toward entry

view toward kitchen

view toward closet zone

view toward balcony and kitchen

view toward west elevation

transverse sectional view

view toward bedroom and roof louvers

view toward roof structure and louvers

Axi:Ome | process framing models

laminated binary form with structural frame

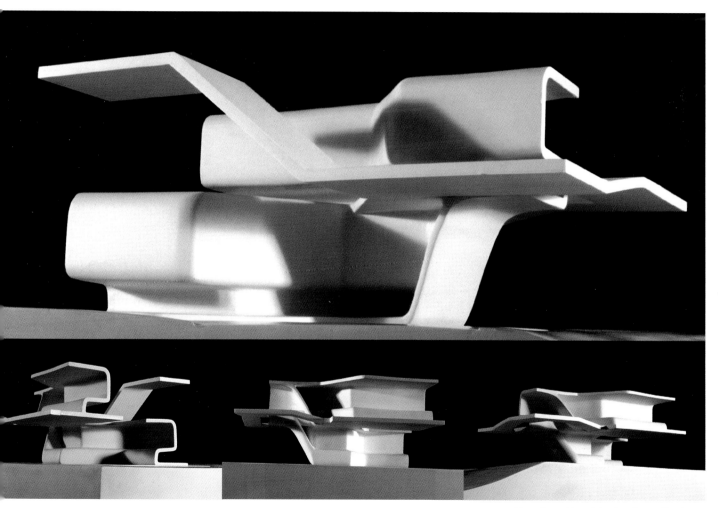

binary form with peripheral surface and landscape

Axi:Ome digital renderings

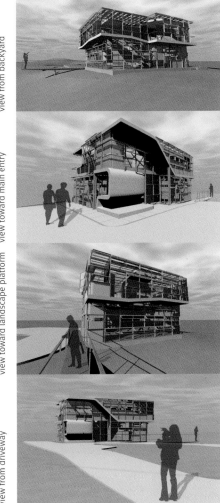

view from backyard

view toward main entry

view toward landscape platform

view from driveway

kitchen

reading area

dining area

library

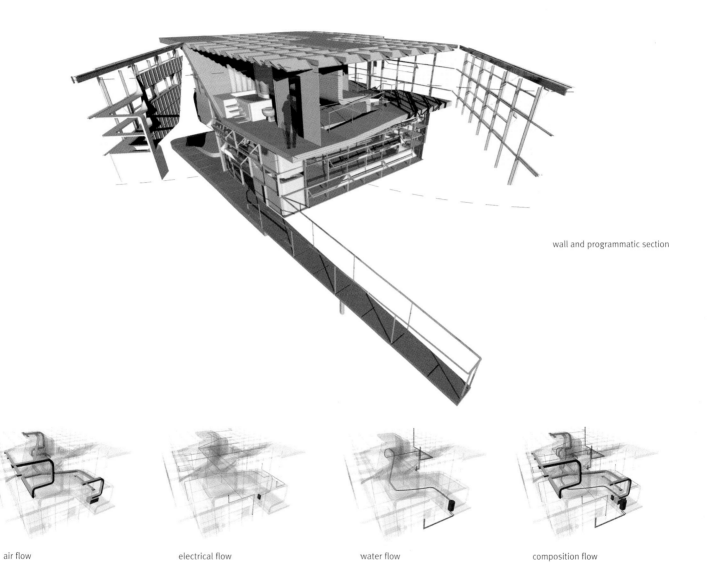

wall and programmatic section

air flow

electrical flow

water flow

composition flow

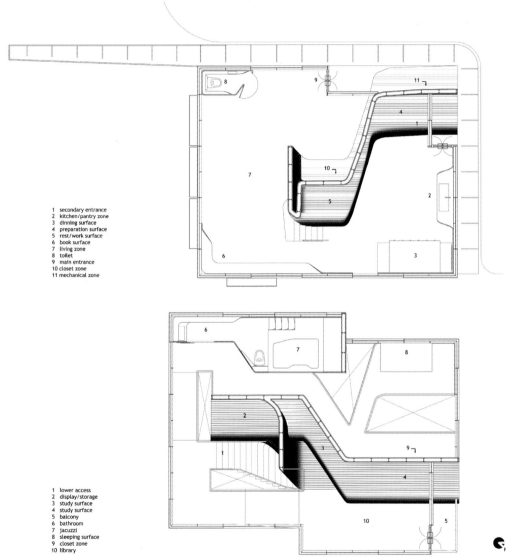

Axi:Ome | floor plans

1 secondary entrance
2 kitchen/pantry zone
3 dinning surface
4 preparation surface
5 rest/work surface
6 book surface
7 living zone
8 toilet
9 main entrance
10 closet zone
11 mechanical zone

1 lower access
2 display/storage
3 study surface
4 study surface
5 balcony
6 bathroom
7 jacuzzi
8 sleeping surface
9 closet zone
10 library

0 1' 2'   5'   10'
N

transverse sections

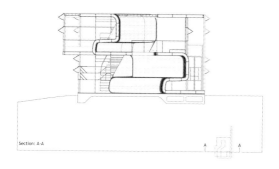

Section: A-A

A A

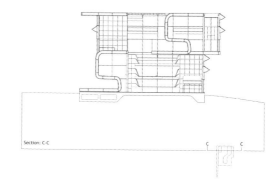

Section: C-C

C C

longitudinal sections

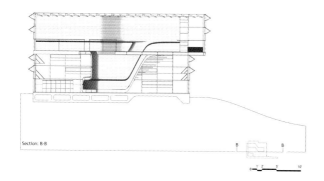

Section: B-B

B B

0 1 2 5' 10'

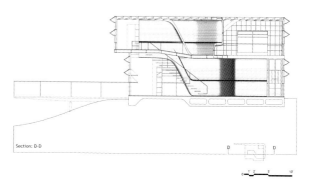

Section: D-D

D D

0 1 2 5' 10'

Axi:Ome | process diagrams

binary form transformation

movement and territorial

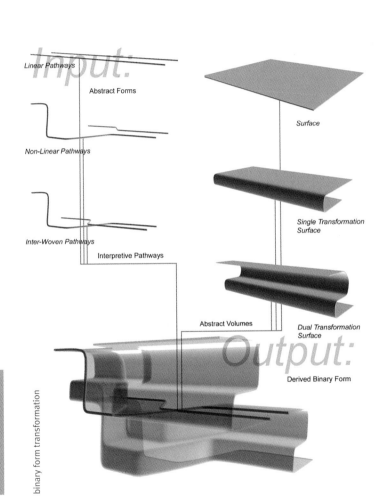

Input:

Linear Pathways

Abstract Forms

Non-Linear Pathways

Inter-Woven Pathways

Interpretive Pathways

Abstract Volumes

Output:

Surface

Single Transformation
Surface

Dual Transformation
Surface

Derived Binary Form

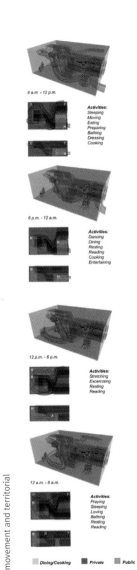

6 a.m. - 12 p.m.

Activities:
*Sleeping
Moving
Eating
Preparing
Bathing
Dressing
Cooking*

6 p.m. - 12 a.m.

Activities:
*Dancing
Dining
Resting
Reading
Cooking
Entertaining*

12 p.m. - 6 p.m.

Activities:
*Stretching
Excercising
Resting
Reading*

12 a.m. - 6 a.m.

Activities:
*Praying
Sleeping
Loving
Bathing
Resting
Reading*

■ *Dining/Cooking*　■ *Private*　■ *Public*

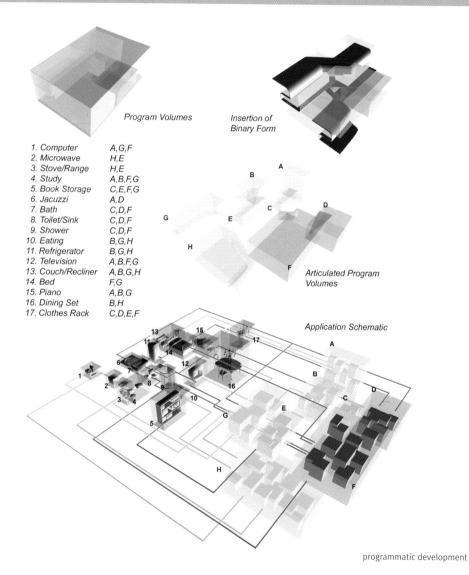

Program Volumes

Insertion of
Binary Form

Articulated Program
Volumes

Application Schematic

1. Computer	A,G,F
2. Microwave	H,E
3. Stove/Range	H,E
4. Study	A,B,F,G
5. Book Storage	C,E,F,G
6. Jacuzzi	A,D
7. Bath	C,D,F
8. Toilet/Sink	C,D,F
9. Shower	C,D,F
10. Eating	B,G,H
11. Refrigerator	B,G,H
12. Television	A,B,F,G
13. Couch/Recliner	A,B,G,H
14. Bed	F,G
15. Piano	A,B,G
16. Dining Set	B,H
17. Clothes Rack	C,D,E,F

programmatic development

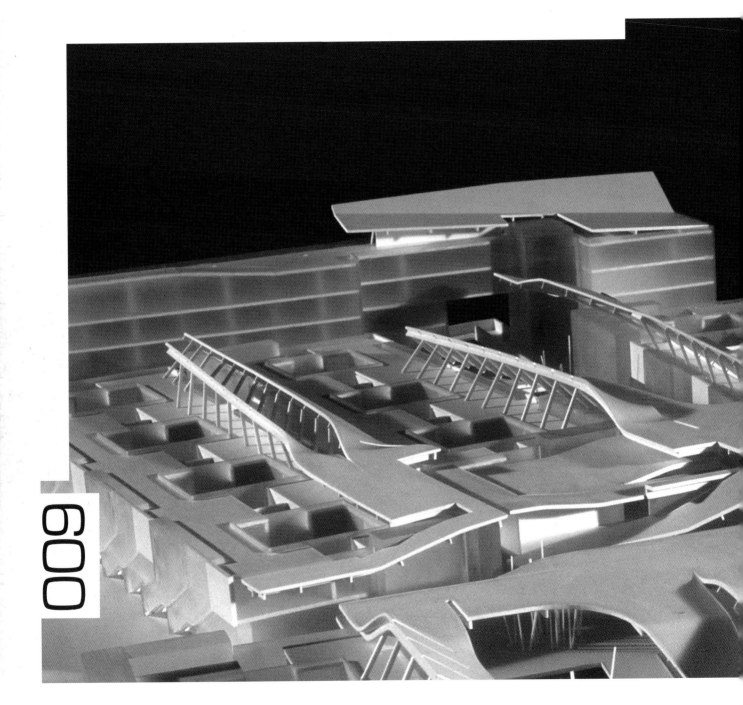

009

AOMORI HOUSING

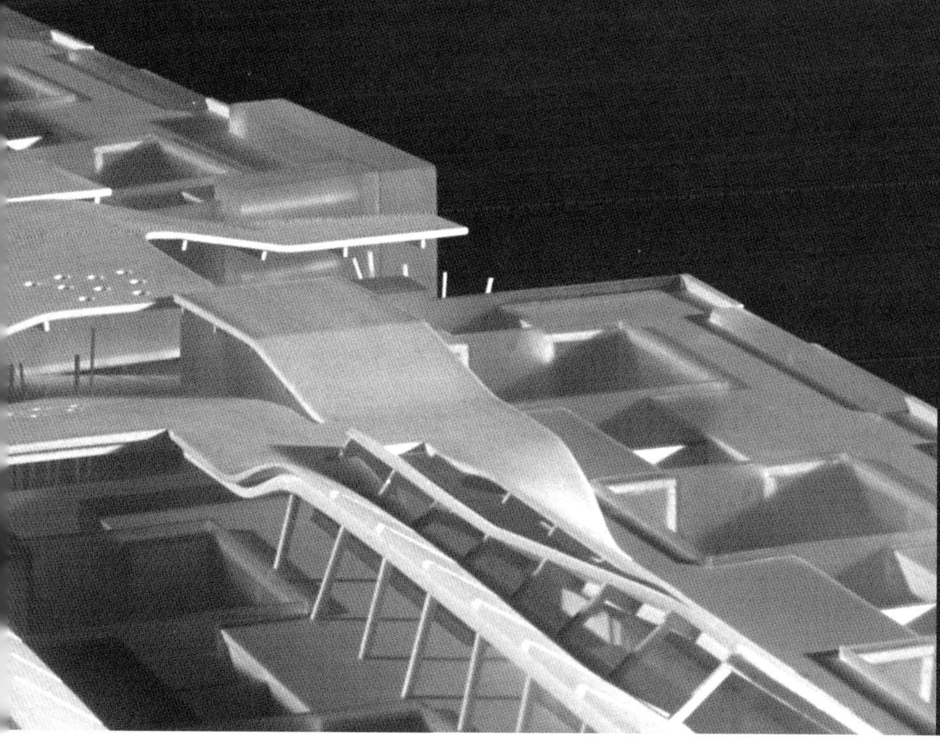

AOMORI:JAPAN

DESIGN PRINCIPALS

sung ho kim with

judith wolin

PROJECT COORDINATORS

christopher rountos

hamis mhando

jeffrey yan

mark stenson

DESIGN TEAM

ahsan najmi

brandon petrella

david constable

egils ramans

george yam

lina sergie

mara noble

paul yam

physical model

Axi:Ome

roofscape view

When the snow comes to Aomori, the neighborhood is sheltered under a thick white blanket. Only the pedestrian street and the courtyards, warmed by heating elements imbedded in the paving, are clear. Cars move freely below the houses and park at the entry to each house. Light enters the garages through the translucent glazed floors of the courts. Each house has an entry room and its own staircase, leading to an L-shaped unit with its own garden. At the edges of the site, taller buildings house apartments served by elevators.

The energy to heat the paths and yards that join the community together comes from photovoltaic canopies above the dwellings and public spaces that also clear themselves of snow. The energy stores in batteries and delivers itself in fine wires similar to those embedded in automobile windows.

The social spaces occur at each end and at the center of the pedestrian street, which connects to the streets beyond the site by ramps and elevators. The community center and bathhouse have entrances at the garage level as well, so that people with limited mobility can reach almost every part of the neighborhood.

There are 200 apartments, each with one parking space: 40 two and three-bedroom duplexes, 70 courtyard apartments, and 90 one-and two-bedroom units served by elevators. At the center of the site there is a bathhouse, a child-care center and a facility for the elderly. On the main avenue there is a cultural hall for movies and lectures, as well as a row of shops. While on the narrow public street, one finds smaller shops and a community meeting room. Although access to the parking level is gated, the movement of the foot traffic into and through the site on the pedestrian (upper) level is continuous with the surrounding web of streets. This way, the houses and pedestrian ways form a blanket over the parking, the snow lays down an insulating blanket over the dwellings and the canopies gather energy from the sun and float above the snow.

Axi:Ome | physical models

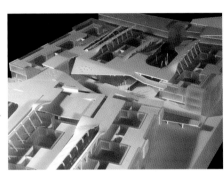

waterfall and pool

elevated ground folding to parking

photovoltaic folding panel controlling light and water runoff

courtyard roofscape

site model

snowfall blanket

view through housing and bathhouse

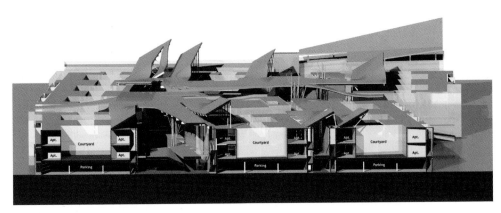

view through housing and courtyard

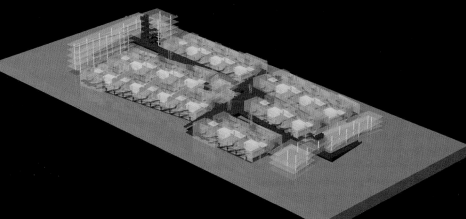

Commercial Zones

Day-Care Center

Bathing Area

Private Courtyards

Community Center

Senior Center

Lecture Hall / Movie Theater

Pedestrian Infrastructure

Axi:Ome   housing unit physical models

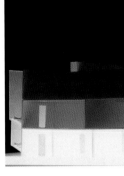
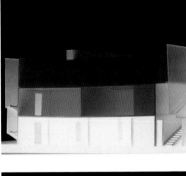

view through entry stairs

view of housing elevation

view through courtyard and parking

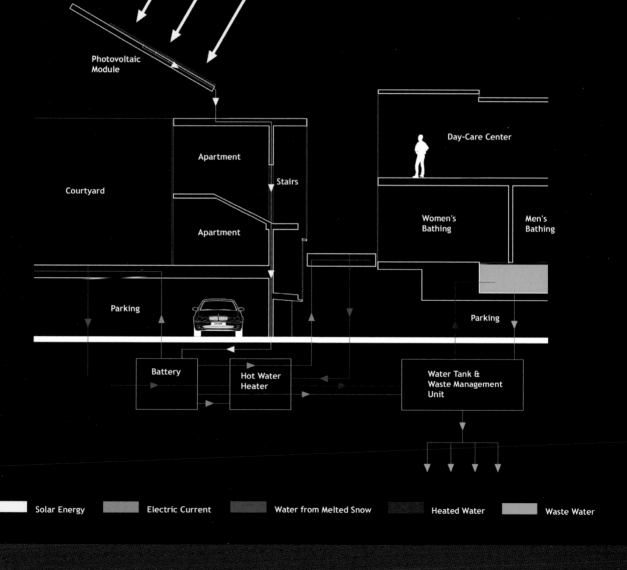

sustainable systems diagram

Photovoltaic Module

Day-Care Center

Courtyard

Apartment

Stairs

Apartment

Women's Bathing

Men's Bathing

Parking

Parking

Battery

Hot Water Heater

Water Tank & Waste Management Unit

Solar Energy   Electric Current   Water from Melted Snow   Heated Water   Waste Water

010

DESIGN PRINCIPALS

sung ho kim with ove arups

PROJECT COORDINATORS

hamis mhando

jihoon kim

DESIGN TEAM

adni isakovic

christopher rountos

lincoln lewis

neena gupta

BANGKOK:THAILAND

OVE ARUPS ENGINEERING TEAM

andrew mole : general oversight

caroline field : meshing guidance and general oversight

darren sault : reanalysis and imaging production

katherine steinhardt : meshing and analysis

mark russin : import and export digital models

ADMOTIV HEADQUARTERS

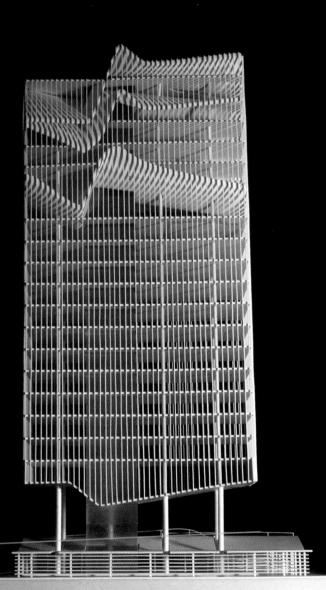

view from the streetscape

Admotiv Headquarters is a 27-story high-rise in the dense and rigid urban site of Bangkok. The building is transformed by the movements, flows, dynamics, and geographic forces of the city's complex urban fabric. The transformation process requires multiple strategies of coordinating the internal spaces by deforming the floor slabs for structural dynamics. The flows of economic, cultural and geographic tectonics shift across the urban field, providing the source of research for the flexible hyper-surfaced floor slabs. According to the geographical research, the site's high groundwater content causes shifting of the structural plates, directing the structural density to occur at the upper levels and leaving the building light as it touches the ground. Height, imaging and programmatic organizations demonstrate a culture of corporate efficiency. In a city with extended working hours, leisure and business bridge one another.

The structural calculations in the vertical sections act as the mechanism to draw one architectural element into another, from floor into wall, from line into surface, from void into solid and from space into program. Admotiv Headquarters opportunistically assembles new forms of media and leisure programs in between the fissures of the hyper-surfaces.

Admotiv Headquarters is a high profile mixed-use building for an international advertisement corporation with influence in new media and information technology. The architecture becomes the agent for urban imaging and branding of marketing prototypes in technological and media development. The headquarters registers and informs its complex geometries through the calibration of unseen forces of economy, technology and materiality of geography.

Axi:0me high-rise physical models

view: southern elevation

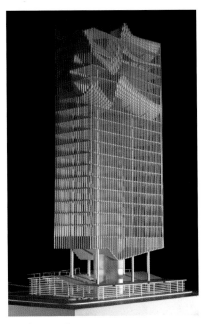

view: hyper-surfacescape

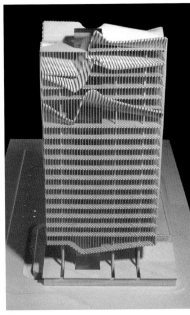

view: roofscape

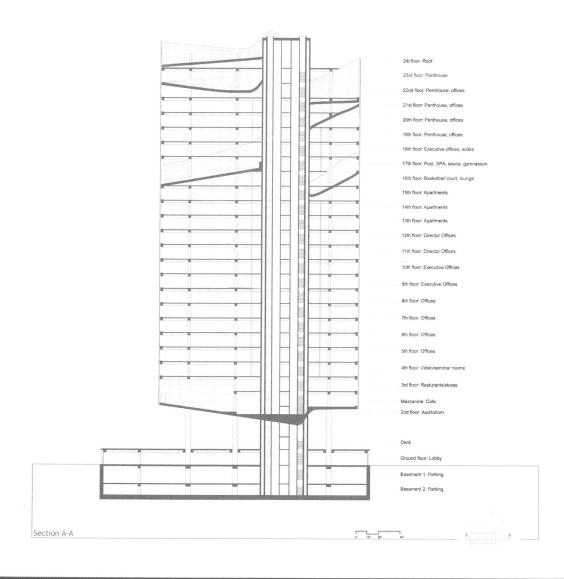

24t floor: Roof

23rd floor: Penthouse

22nd floor: Penthouse, offices

21st floor: Penthouse, offices

20th floor: Penthouse, offices

19th floor: Penthouse, offices

18th floor: Executive offices, suites

17th floor: Pool, SPA, sauna, gymnasium

16th floor: Basketball court, lounge

15th floor: Apartments

14th floor: Apartments

13th floor: Apartments

12th floor: Director Offices

11th floor: Director Offices

10th floor: Executive Offices

9th floor: Executive Offices

8th floor: Offices

7th floor: Offices

6th floor: Offices

5th floor: Offices

4th floor: Video/seminar rooms

3rd floor: Resturants/stores

Mezzanine: Cafe

2nd floor: Auditorium

Deck

Ground floor: Lobby

Basement 1: Parking

Basement 2: Parking

Section A-A

0'   10'   20'   40'

compressed private
spatial volume

compressed public
spatial volume

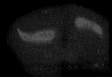

compressed multi-functional
spatial volume

dual spatial insertion

dual spatial enfold

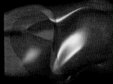

spatial matrix flows

floor slab levels

+21.0 floor
+20.0 floor
+19.0 floor
+18.0 floor
+17.0 floor
+16.0 floor
+15.0 floor
+14.0 floor
+13.0 floor
+12.0 floor
+11.0 floor
+10.0 floor
+9.0 floor
+8.0 floor
+7.0 floor
+6.0 floor
+5.0 floor
+4.0 floor
+3.0 floor
+2.0 floor
+1.0 floor

0.0 floor
-1.0 floor
-2.0 floor

finite element structural analysis

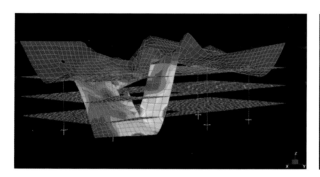 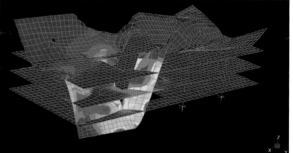

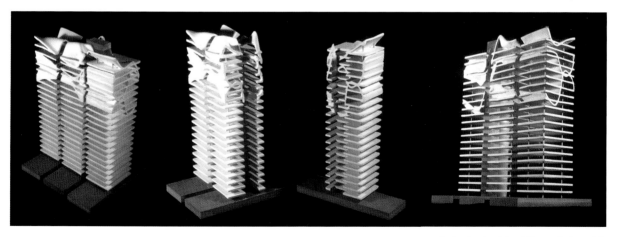

plaster structural simulation analysis models

component diagrams

Axi:Ome

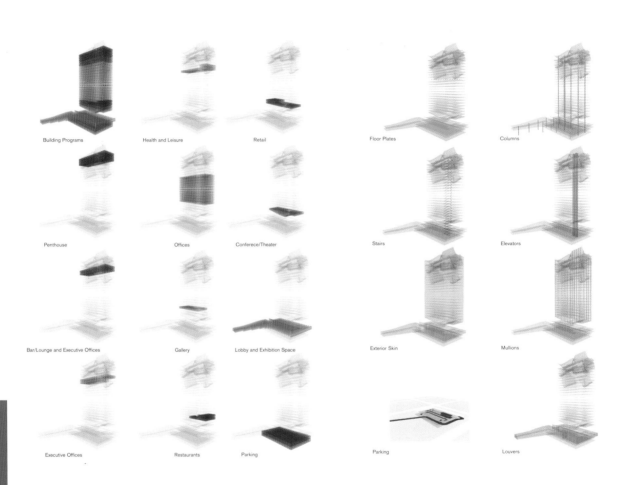

Building Programs

Health and Leisure

Retail

Floor Plates

Columns

Penthouse

Offices

Conferece/Theater

Stairs

Elevators

Bar/Lounge and Executive Offices

Gallery

Lobby and Exhibition Space

Exterior Skin

Mullions

Executive Offices

Restaurants

Parking

Parking

Louvers

programmatic components

building components

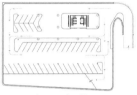

underground parking
level 01

3rd floor

19th floor

ground floor-lobby
level 1

5th thru 14th floors

20th floor

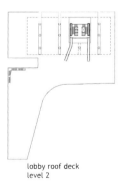

lobby roof deck
level 2

15th floor

21st floor

N

events renderings

Axi:0me

office space

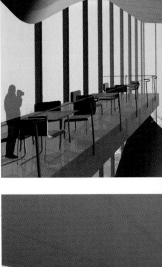

penthouse

climbing wall

conference space

penthouse

pool

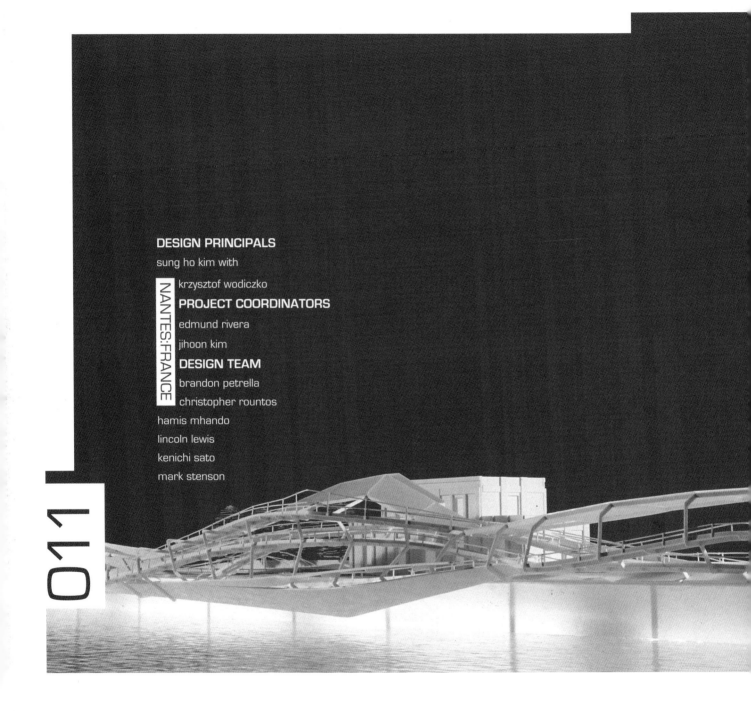

DESIGN PRINCIPALS

sung ho kim with

krzysztof wodiczko

PROJECT COORDINATORS

edmund rivera

jihoon kim

DESIGN TEAM

brandon petrella

christopher rountos

hamis mhando

lincoln lewis

kenichi sato

mark stenson

NANTES:FRANCE

011

SLAVERY MEMORIAL

physical site model

Axi:Ome

aerial view toward event surfaces

The site of the Slavery Memorial was once the processing depot for millions of African and Caribbean slaves. This was the location for distribution, where people were traded, branded and dispersed without any acknowledgement of humanity aside from the recording of retail information. The Slavery Memorial is a vessel of memory-scapes and data-fields for the forgotten culture of slavery. The structure mediates between land and sea by oscillating between the horizontality and the expansion of the urban growth on the site by merging history into the horizon. The memorial levitates above the ground and generates zones of horizontal banding across the site. The bands define historical information and differentiated public garden surfaces. The fluctuating terrain of sculpture gardens occupies the collage of history between the folds of the shifting bands and combines the two realms of public and memorial space.

The memorial spaces are activated at night by a transforming spectrum of lights, media and sound linking the city with the public pedestrian flows. The public space acts as an urban observation deck uncovering the cultural and economic development of the city through the water ports. The memorial engulfs and grafts series of surfaces on the existing historical building in order to interface the past with the present. Constructed with the same precision as the bow of a ship, the memorial vessel attaches to the edge of the water site. Through different seasons, the water seeps through the vessel in such a manner that parts of the spaces are submerged. Event surfaces allow gatherings for celebration of marginalized cultures. The Slavery Memorial is a vital space and a place for sustaining cultural memory in the contemporary world.

physical site models

Axi:0me

urban pathways and urban decks

flow of water, people and history

flow of media, energy and sound

folds of shifting bands of event surfaces

interface between land and water

memorial surfaces: grafting
existing historical building

process models

Axi:Ome

banding articulation

site interface

light movement

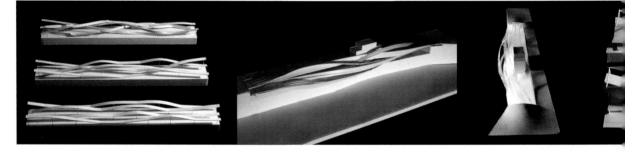

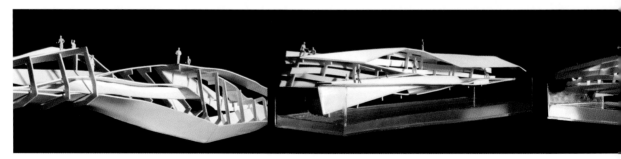

memorial vessel: view 2

walking surfaces

structure and surface   urban deck and memorial interface   memorial vessel: view 1

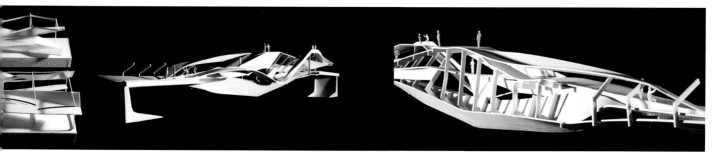

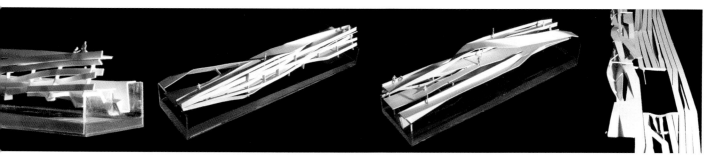

media facades   pedestrian and water interface : view 1   pedestrian and water interface : view 2   site bandings process models

Axi:Ome

transversal sectional models

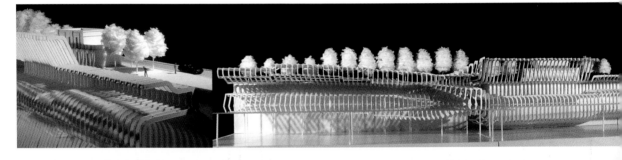

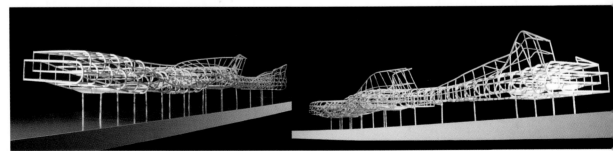

woven structural models

vertical deformation model

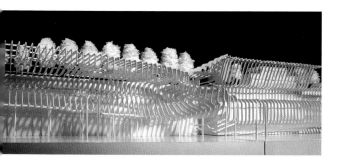

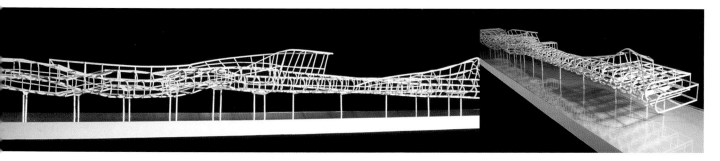

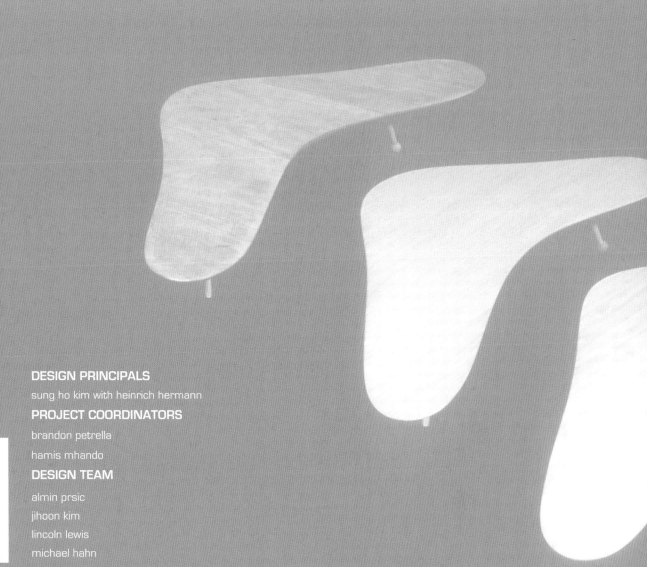

DESIGN PRINCIPALS
sung ho kim with heinrich hermann
PROJECT COORDINATORS
brandon petrella
hamis mhando
DESIGN TEAM
almin prsic
jihoon kim
lincoln lewis
michael hahn

NOGUCHI TABLE

The Noguchi Table project recreates the lost geometry of an original Isamu Noguchi Table burned in a fire. By analyzing the photos (representational images), multiple diagrammatic and mapping procedures were invented to observe the proportions, profiles and dimensions of the table in its original space. From the 2-D investigations, physical 3-D models were built to understand the materiality and contextual processes. The physical models were then cut in different axis sections, scanned into a computer, and reconstructed through digital modeling. In return, the virtual tool articulated the physical process and allowed more fluid research into the manufacturing of the Noguchi Table.

In addition to finding lost geometry, the Noguchi Table research develops a reverse engineering process that allows existing photographs to be mapped onto 3-D digital modeling software. Computers construct the geometry by building a digital model of the room and the space where the table was located in the house, including the table, the floor patterns, the windows and the doors—those elements acting as a reference point to define the basic geometry of the table. Solely constructing the model digitally became too abstract, so the physical models construct material sensibility in shaping the form of the table using a touch of handcrafting. By cutting and creating models on different axes, we obtain the sectional curves that may then be scanned back into a computer to negotiate with the digital model. For the final manufacturing drawings, the shipbuilding carpenter works with full-scale templates—reconstructing the geometry through template and by hand.

chris genter

Axi:Ome

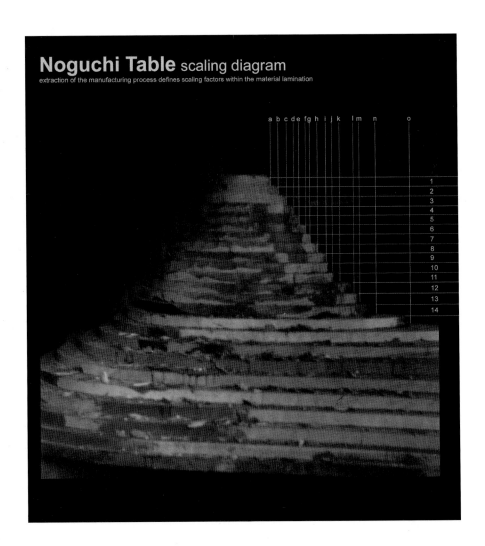

Noguchi Table scaling diagram

extraction of the manufacturing process defines scaling factors within the material lamination

Recently Axi:Ome was commissioned to re-create the geometry of a dining table designed by Isamu Noguchi for the residence of William Burden. The original table and drawings were destroyed, so its form was interpolated from photographs. This table, like many of the projects in this book, bears only a slight resemblance to the familiar. More similar to the hull of a boat or a boomerang than a table, Noguchi was not interested in simply replicating or even restyling a familiar object, but in exploring its formal and spatial possibilities. The table's contours both shape and are shaped by the curved room and ocean landscape in which it is situated. He does not begin with the table, but with the idea of an object in the room, which must accommodate certain activities—eating, gathering—and uses the opportunity to choreograph light, movement and space with shape: "If sculpture is the rock, it is also the space between the rock and a man, and the communication and contemplation between." This table is an enquiry into the effects of shape—its ability to effect sight, movement, action and ultimately thought.

A 1949 article, "The Art of Spaces," suggests that these new shapes are a response to changes in the way that the world is intellectually constructed: "Indeed we can no longer escape the questions posed by the intrusion of science upon our changing awareness of reality. It is as much the creation of man's imaginings as were our ancient myths. The need is for its integration within ourselves—the challenge to the artist is that of giving it shape." The response is equally emotional:

> Our reaction to the physical environment may be represented as a series of hazy but continuous aesthetic judgments. Such judgments affect even the control of our emotions, bringing order out of chaos, a myth out of the world, a sense of belonging out of our loneliness. Likewise, through the familiarity and understanding of formal and tactile relationships, we acquire an appreciation of the invention of nature and man. Hence, any change in the emotional climate of our environment becomes a matter of artistic consideration.

In both cases, the act of creating new forms seeks to generate meaning, and in so doing integrates us with an environment from which we have become estranged.

In my mind, the work of Axi:Ome is similarly motivated, seeking to translate contemporary experience into relevant, dynamic objects that can both generate meaning and affect physical and intellectual change. Consequently, much like Noguchi's table, these buildings respond to the conditions of their immediate perception, use and construction, instead of conforming to conventional ideas of form or practice. The key to this approach is an understanding of architecture as composed of activity, of motion. Inherited architectural languages and forms are discarded as a departure point for thinking about built form. Instead, projects begin with an analysis of forces operating in the project, whether it be the environmental—sun, wind—cultural, technical, or physical—anticipated behaviors of a human body in a given space or situation. This analysis typically provides a series of diagrams in two and three dimensions that function as a set of maps or operating instructions for giving shape to material. Physical modeling translates these abstract diagrams into possible architectures; surfaces are warped, folded, bent and twisted to accommodate, control, or resist forces. This might sound more like the design process for an airplane wing or a ship's hull. But unlike these, Axi:Ome's primary consideration is perceptions —the way in which this form interacts with the body and the mind.

The Book House, for example, is approached as a series of activities and the relationship of these to the movement of the sun through the course of the day. Instead of defining the house as a series of rooms, it is understood as a kind of choreography. The building materializes from the movement of the body through time. This idea of the body as a physical, shape—giving and space-defining force was explored by the modern choreographer Martha Graham, who collaborated with Noguchi and influenced his ideas of space. Graham would wrap dancers in a sheet of fabric that expanded and contracted and was given shape by the explosive motions of the body inside it. In the Book House, a continuous surface, like this piece of fabric, interacts with the body,

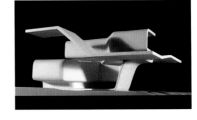

008 : book house

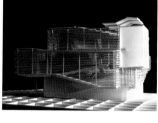

001 : parallel church

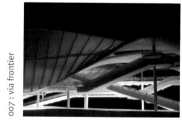

007 : via frontier

011 : slavery memorial

twisting and bending in response to its anticipated movements. What results is a fluid, dynamic space that is not meant to be understood simply intellectually, but also physically. Such changes in our physical experience have profound effects —a heightened awareness of the body, of the physical environment, and of our relationships in the world.

It is tempting, seeing this work as a series of images in a book, to understand it as abstract form-making, as the stylistic fancy of an architect's theoretical work. However, this architecture advocates a return to the body and to the physical world as primary sites for architectural creation. It is not a stylistic quest, but the language of curved and warped surfaces that has evolved reflects an attempt to materialize the forces that exist in a place or situation, and in so doing open them up to experience and reflection. It is critical, then, to use these shapes as instruments to understand and to experience these forces. Arguably, the Book House is a straightforward example in which physical movements effect a surface. Projects like the Parallel Church—which seeks to give shape to spiritual forces —or the Via Frontier Mall (retail forces), or the Slavery Memorial (cultural forces), are more complex in that they are not direct translations of physical actions to shape. But each uses shape to make the latent apparent. I would challenge you to look back at these works and to confront them not as images but as navigational tools. Put your body into these works, and, like Noguchi's table, they will change the way you move, see, and think.

Axi:Ome photo-grafting

digital model overlay on family photo

noguchi table model with eames plywood chairs

Axi:Ome | process models

lamination model

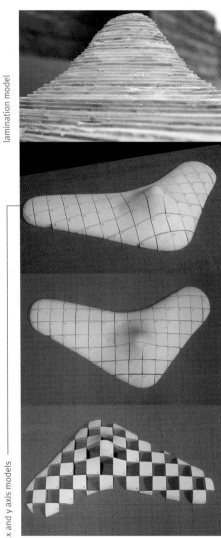

x and y axis models

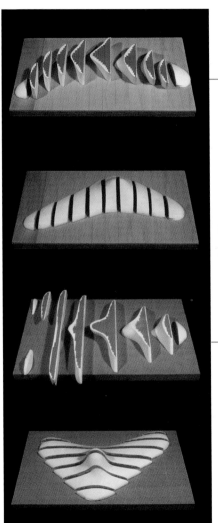

x axis models

y axis models

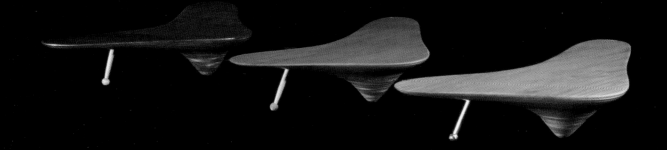

photo-grafting

digital model overlays on photos: belly geometries

parametric surface models

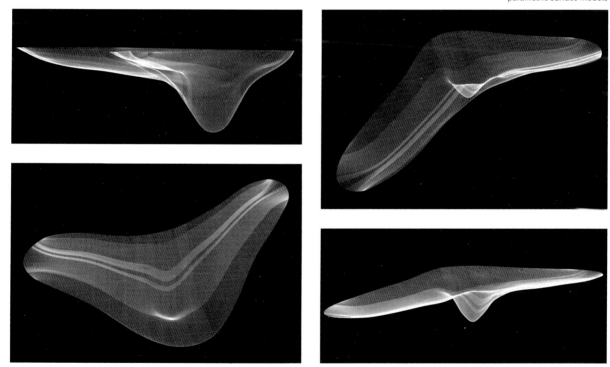

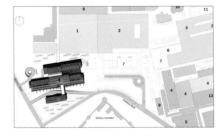

Project 013: Osaka Master Plan
Osaka: Japan

Design Principals: Sung Ho Kim and Pablo Rozenwasser

Project 014: Moscow Hotel
Moscow: Russia

Design Principals: Sung Ho Kim and Paul Donnelly

Client: KECO investment, engineering, development GMBH

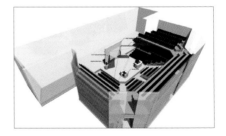

Project 018: 3200 Locust Office
St. Louis: Mo

Design Principals-in-Charge:
Heather Woofter and Sung Ho Kim

Client: Wade Paschall

Project 019: Secret Stage Set
St. Louis: Mo

Design Principals-in-Charge:
Heather Woofter and Sung Ho Kim

Client: St. Louis Community College Forest Park Theater

Project 015: Grand Center Urban Mediascape
St. Louis: Mo

Design Principals-in-Charge:
Heather Woofter and Sung Ho Kim

Client: Friedman Group Ltd.

Project 016: Amonte House
St. Louis: Mo

Design Principals-in-Charge:
Heather Woofter and Sung Ho Kim

Client: Metropolitan Design & Building

Project 017: Glass House
Catawba Valley: Va

Design Principals-in-Charge:
Heather Woofter and Sung Ho Kim

Client: Cynthia and David Woofter

Project 020: Women's Shelter
St. Louis: Mo

Design Principals-in-Charge:
Heather Woofter and Sung Ho Kim

Client: Father Dempsey

Project 021: Urban Gallery
St. Louis: Mo

Design Principals-in-Charge:
Heather Woofter and Sung Ho Kim

Client: Art St. Louis

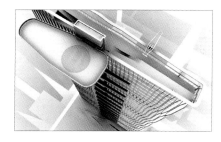

Project 022: Carbon Fiber Tower
Bangkok: Thailand

Design Principals-in-Charge: Heather Woofter
and Sung Ho Kim

Client: Media Reflex Co. Ltd

Erdem Erten received his BArch from Middle East Technical University, and his SMArchS and PhD from Massachusetts Institute of Technology. His research focuses on 19th and 20th century Architecture and Urbanism, and 18th and 19th century British Aesthetic Theory and Landscape Architecture. He is currently an Assistant Professor of Architecture at Izmir Institute of Technology in Turkey.

Christopher Genter received his BArch from Cornell University and his SMArchS from Massachusetts Institute of Technology. He has worked for Machado and Silvetti Associates, Inc. in Boston and Renzo Piano Building Workshop in Genoa. He is currently a Lecturer of Architecture at Northeastern University.

Stuart Steck received his BA from Cornell University, his MA from Boston University and is currently a PhD candidate researching the works of Ellsworth Kelly. He has taught art history and critical theory at Brown University, Suffolk University, Art Institute of Boston, Boston University, Massachusetts Institute of Technology and is currently an Assistant Professor at The Art Institute of Boston at Lesley University.

Lynnette Widder received her BA from Barnard College and her MArch from Columbia University. She was the editor for the architectural journal Daidalos and has lectured and published extensively on contemporary architecture internationally. She has taught at Federal Technical Institute, University of British Columbia, Cornell University, and Columbia University. She has practiced in Europe and in the United States and is a principal of Aadvarchitecture in New York City. She is the recipient of a Fulbright Scholarship, as well as grants from the Kinne Fund and the Rhode Island School of Design. Currently she is an Associate Professor and the Head of the Architecture Department at Rhode Island School of Design.

Heather Woofter received her BArch from Virginia Tech and her MArch from Harvard University. She has practiced in the United States and the United Kingdom as a licensed architect and presented at numerous international conferences on architectural education. She has taught at Boston Architectural College, Roger Williams University and was an Assistant Professor of Architecture at Virginia Tech. She is currently a design principal of Axi:Ome llc and an Assistant Professor at Washington University in St. Louis where she coordinates the graduate core program.

Tina Yuan received her BS in Graphic Design from California Polytechnic State University in San Luis Obispo. She has worked in San Francisco and New York and has been the Coordinator of Graphic Media for Axi:Ome llc in various mediums and processes (web, publication, branding, logo). She is currently a designer for Design Within Reach.

This book is in memory of my father Sin Jang Kim

I would like to thank those who made Spatial Practice possible: Heather Woofter for making so many things in my life possible and for her love and unconditional support. Tina Yuan, for her endless dedication to the design of the book over the past three years. I am very grateful to Washington University in St. Louis, Sam Fox School of Design and Visual Arts (Dean Carmon Colangelo), J.E. Novack Construction Company (Aaron and Neal Novack), Nancy and Kenneth Kranzberg, Emily Rauh Pulitzer and Kromm, Rikimaru & Johansen (Young Hie and David Kromm), for making the publication of the book financially possible. Special thanks to the talent and dedication of Axi:Ome Providence (Jeffrey Yan, Kelly Driscoll, Egils Ramans, Sehzat Oner, and Lincoln Lewis), and Axi:Ome St. Louis (Jihoon Kim, Hamis Mhando, Adni Isakovic, and Geoff Loo): without them there would be no Spatial Practice. My extended thanks to Erdem Erten, Lynnette Widder, Stuart Steck, and Chris Genter for their critical voices and support.

Thank you to Heinrich Hermann, Judith Wolin and Krzysztof Wodiczko for sharing their ideas, thoughts and experiences. It was Philip Parker, Nader Tehrani, Nasrine Seraji, and Duke Reiter who inspired and trained me for Axi:Ome. They all have been my mentors.

In Providence, RI it was Elizabeth Dean Hermann, Silvia Acosta, Anne Tate, Michelle Fornabai, Robert O'Neal, and Peter Tagiuri who believed in the work with great support. In Cambridge, MA it was Ann and John Vollman-Bible, Edith Ackermann, Michael Leja, Hisham Bizri, Omar Khan, Laura Garofalo, Warren Sack, Ellen Dunham-Jones and Ann Pendleton-Jullian, who gave support and criticism along the way. In St. Louis, MO it was Paul Donnelly, Eric Mumford, Stephen Leet and Gia Daskalakis who were great friends and supporters of Axi:Ome.

On a personal note, I would like to thank my mother Min Ja Kim and sister Sung Hee Nee for always being the pillars of my life. Todd Leong for his collaboration throughout the years and for financially jump starting Axi:Ome Providence, and Barbra Leong for her support. To my friends and collaborators Adam Whiton, Bryant Yeh and Margot Krasso-Krasojevic for sharing their expertise and knowledge. Also to Nancy and Aaron Novack, for their friendship and support that has verged on sponsorship. To Kenneth Kranzberg for his vision and Emily Pulitzer for her wisdom and trust.

I would like to thank Gabriel Feld, George Thrush, Cynthia Weese, and Bruce Lindsey for allowing me to develop Axi:Ome through academic settings and processes. Finally to my students from Rhode Island School of Design, Northeastern University and Washington University in St. Louis who have dedicated their lives to the discipline of architecture that has been the inspiration for Axi:Ome. Without them there would be no future of architecture.

Design team 2000 to 2005

Chris Alonso/RISD - - - - - - - Lori Apfel/Washington University in St. Louis - - - - - - - - Roger Bechtiger/RISD - - - - - - - David Constable/RISD - -

Craig Cosper/Washington University in St. Louis - - - - - - - - - Kelly Driscoll/RISD - - - - - - - - - Joe Duignan/Washington University in St. Louis

Billy Garcia/Washington University in St. Louis - - - - Molly Gleason/RISD - - - - Cheng He Guan/Washington University in St. Louis - - - - Neena Gupta

Michael Hahn - - - Maria-Anna Hatziliades/Northeastern University - - - - Matt Horvath/Washington University in St. Louis - - - - Tyson Hosmer/Virginia Tech

Adni Isakovic/Washington University in St. Louis - - - - DJ Kim/Virginia Tech - - - - Gyu Youl Kim - - - - Jihoon Kim/Washington University in St. Louis - -

Jin Kim/RISD - - - - - Jenny Kwon/Washington University in St. Louis - - - - - Si Eun Lee/Drury University - - - - - Lincoln Lewis/University of Kansas - -

Geoff Loo/Washington University in St. Louis - - - - - - - - - - Pak-kei Mak/RISD - - - - - - - - - Hamis Mhando/Washington University in St. Louis - -

Marisa Miller/Washngton University in St.Louis - - - - Kevin Myers/Washington University in St. Louis - - - - Ahsan Najmi/RISD - - - - Mara Noble/RISD

Sehzat Oner/RISD - Rodrigo Pantoja/Drury University - Brandon Petrella/Northeastern University - Jonathan Powell/Washington University in St. Louis - -

Egils Ramans/RISD - - - - - - - - - Edmund Rivera/Washington University in St. Louis - - - - - - - - Aaron Robin/Washington University in St. Louis - -

Christopher Rountos/Northeastern University - - - - - - Almin Prisc/RISD - - - - - - - Steven Sanderson/Virginia Tech - - - - - - - Kenichi Sato/RISD

Molly Seguto/RISD - - - Lina Sergie/MIT - - - Justin Shaw/Washington University in St. Louis - - - Michael Steinberg/Washington University in St. Louis

Mark W. Stenson/Northeastern University - - Nick Taylor - - Hedieh Wojgani/RISD - George Yam/Nottingham University - Paul Yam - Jeffrey Yan/RISD - -

Sponsors

Nancy and Kenneth Kranzberg - - Emily Rauh Pulitzer

Young Hie and David Kromm

Washington University in St.Louis
SAM FOX SCHOOL OF DESIGN & VISUAL ARTS

J.E. Novack
Construction Company

Axi:Ome